OUT OF THIS WORLD

South West Poets

Edited by Jenni Bannister

First published in Great Britain in 2015 by:

Young**Writers**

Remus House
Coltsfoot Drive
Peterborough
PE2 9BF
Telephone: 01733 890066
Website: www.youngwriters.co.uk

Printed and bound in the UK by BookPrintingUK
Website: www.bookprintinguk.com

FOREWORD

Here at Young Writers our defining aim is to promote the joys of reading and writing to children and young adults and we are committed to nurturing the creative talents of the next generation. By allowing them to see their own work in print we believe their confidence and love of creative writing will grow.

Out Of This World is our latest fantastic competition, specifically designed to encourage the writing skills of primary school children through the medium of poetry. From the high quality of entries received, it is clear that it really captured the imagination of all involved.

We are proud to present the resulting collection of poems that we are sure will amuse and inspire.

An absorbing insight into the imagination and thoughts of the young, we hope you will agree that this fantastic anthology is one to delight the whole family again and again.

CONTENTS

THE POEMS

Look At The Sky

Just look at the sky
See the planets fly by
The wonderful sight that meets the eye
See all the stars way up high

Mercury number one
Hotter than a gun
Venus number two
Makes you feel good
Earth number three
Tour it then you'll see
Mars number four
Just watch it soar
Jupiter comes five
You and I can't survive!
Saturn on six
With the rings that create a good mix
Uranus up on seven
As blue as Heaven
Neptune number eight
You just can't hate
Pluto number nine
But now over time
It's not considered a planet anymore
Because of its size and the way it soars

Just look at the sky
The wonderful sight that meets the eye!

Habeebah Patel (10)
Al-Ashraf Primary School, Gloucester

Exploration Space

Up and up through the dark sky
Among the many dusty galaxies lies the spiral Milky Way
In the three dimensional space where there is no gravitational pull
Lies the gigantic solar system
Gas, flames, bursting bright is the colourful sun of orange, yellow and red
Pulled by its gravitational pull causing orbit of the planetary system
Mercury, Venus, Earth and Mars
Jupiter, Saturn, Uranus and Neptune
The eight main planets of which Earth is our home
Consisting of life, our food and water
Kept in position by the downward gravitational pull
The Earth spins on its axis, tilted at 23.5 degrees
Taking 365 days to orbit the sun
To Earth there is one moon
Which has no water, wind or air
It is dark but shows a bright reflection round or crescent shaped
Full of craters or rocks and glass
The first man onto the moon known as Neil Armstrong
Who wore a white space suit
And travelled into space on a spacecraft
Hereafter many rockets, astronauts, spacecraft followed
So if someday you get a chance
Grab a telescope and take a glance
Look up high into the sky
Into the wonders of outer space.

Esmail Salehbhai (9)
Al-Ashraf Primary School, Gloucester

Solar System In My View

Mercury is very sweltering
You'll melt, you'll burn and you'll find no sheltering
Venus is a hottie
Like a warm chapati
Mars is like a red chocolate bar
It looks like a luminous shooting star
Jupiter flies around like Zeus
Personally I think it looks like a moose
Saturn and its rings
Beauty it does bring
Uranus is very cloudy
Inhabitants would be rowdy
The eighth planet is Neptune
From germs it is immune
Pluto is very dwarf
It's gone through a million morphs

Let's talk about Earth
The mother that gave birth
To life as we know
Summer, spring, rain and snow
There is no other like it, planet one or ten
Earth is truly the solar system's gem.

Hamza Surty (9)
Al-Ashraf Primary School, Gloucester

Space

Space, space there is no weight,
You can all be lightweight champions in space.
Pluto, Pluto the planet that made
Us listen to the radio
Because apparently it's a dwarf planet.
Neptune, Neptune the planet that makes
Your nephew puzzled.
Which one is the god and which one is the planet?
Uranus, Uranus, just about
Fits in the universe. Oh what a
Really big planet.
Saturn, Saturn has rings
With patterns.
I feel like walking on the
Very smooth rings.
The biggest planet of all,
Jupiter, Jupiter makes gas giants
Look like a junior, junior.
There is a big difference
Between Jupiter and
The other planets.

Talha Jeewa (9)
Al-Ashraf Primary School, Gloucester

Space And Beyond

It is a new world out there
And a brand new affair.
There might be species of life
For all we know they may use a butter knife.
The stars are our goal
Only then we will be whole.
To the stars and beyond
Seeing little ponds.
Where will the stars take me?
Will I ever be free?
There is a big black hole
And a long star pole
The cosmos and galaxies out there are more than a million
Maybe more than a billion.
Will I ever survive?
I want to be alive.
In the depths of space
A whole new frontier
With a lot of fear.

Mohammed Patel (10)
Al-Ashraf Primary School, Gloucester

I Look Up From Earth

Earth is our everlasting home
Which we will roam.
I look up from Earth and try to see
The planets looking back at me.
I gaze at bright and distant stars
And try to see Mercury or Mars.

I squint at the Milky Way, way up high
And look for Jupiter in the sky.
Where are Saturn, Uranus, Venus and Neptune?
They are far away, high like the moon.
A telescope would be the best to spot Pluto and the rest.

There are nine planets that orbit the sun
But humans and animals just live on one.
Earth is our planet, we must take good care
Of the air, land and water we must share.
Astronauts travel a long way through space
And they learn facts which they bring back to us.
I look up from the Earth.

Ali Imran (9)
Al-Ashraf Primary School, Gloucester

Twinkle Star

Twinkle, twinkle, little star
Very bright and very far
In the sky like a tiny dot
Glowing gas that's very hot
Twinkle, twinkle little star
Very bright and very far.

Glowing, glowing, little moon
Like a massive white balloon
Round and round the Earth you spin
Throughout the month, new shapes you're in
Glowing, glowing little moon
Like a massive white balloon.

Bright, bright, red-hot sun
Shining light on everyone
Earth goes round you once a year
You're a star with an atmosphere
Bright, bright red-hot sun
Shining light on everyone!

Asiya Patel (10)
Al-Ashraf Primary School, Gloucester

Outer Space

Space is a big vast place
With lots of planets which are;

Mercury: The closest to the sun
And the hottest planet in our solar system
With really high temperatures.

Venus: The brightest planet in our solar system.
We can see it bright from Earth
If we look in the sky at night.

Earth: The only planet inhabited with humans
Used to be very tall and big.

Mars: The only planet which scientists think
Had life because it has ice caps.

Although this looks like a fact file,
It is still a poem you know by a mile.

This poem about space
Is really just the base.

Mohammed Tahir Mahmood (10)
Al-Ashraf Primary School, Gloucester

Mercury

Mercury am I, gentle, soft
Sixth planet, I send the winds aloft
When other stars are warm, I'm hot;
I'm just as cold when they are not
The twins and the maid so fine
Are the houses I account as mine
In which I go most cleverly
So Jupiter can't bewilder me
I'm at my best when in the maid
But in the fishes sure to fade
Through all the signs I make my ways
In three hundred and four and thirty days.

Rayhan Vahed (9)
Al-Ashraf Primary School, Gloucester

The Universe

Twinkle, twinkle
Sparkle, sparkle
Glitter, glitter
My favourite planet is Jupiter
This gas giant
With beautiful rings
Looks like a ballerina that's gonna sing
La la la la la la la la la la la la
Uranus is blue
It has twenty-seven moons
It is an ice giant
So have a nice forty years sleep
Beep, beep, beep
Then I went to the moon
I felt like I was a kangaroo
I saw aliens that spoke in Urdu
They used to shoot me with a water gun!

Haudane Hassan Omar (10)
Al-Ashraf Primary School, Gloucester

Snow

Look at the pretty snowflakes
Floating slowly to the ground
Like shimmering crystals
Gathering all around

Look at the silent streets
Covered in a blanket of snow
Everyone feeling snuggly and warm
In their favourite throw

Look at the sad lovely snowman
With his pointy carrot nose
Waiting for the children
To play with him as it snows.

Uzma Ahmed (10)
Al-Ashraf Primary School, Gloucester

Attractive Space

Sitting under the big blue sky
But what lies above and beyond?
No gravity in space
So no time to waste
Revolve, rotate and drift away
Tempting, fetching
This amazing spectacle
Is this where I want to be?
Mind-boggling, intriguing
Is the creation of my Creator
Stars gleaming bright
Glimmer, shimmer and shine
All through the night
Blazing sun, relaxing moon
Fulfilling its duty at the command of my, your own Lord
His power, His sovereign has much to testify
Can we really deny?

Aaisha Garda (10)
Al-Ashraf Primary School, Gloucester

The Sun

The sun is a star
And only at night
Will the sun go so far
So far out of sight

It comes back in the morning
Shining as bright as ever
The weather has stopped pouring
And the windows shining like leather

It's time for the sun to set
But it's coming back tomorrow
I'll set you a bet
It's coming back tomorrow.

Sulaiman Ouiles (9)
Al-Ashraf Primary School, Gloucester

Beyond Earth

I see the stars in the sky
Sparkling brightly up so high
I see an astronaut
Floating around the planets just as he was taught
There are nine planets as we all know
Round and round the sun they go
Rockets flying out to space
Rockets flying every place
Gravity keeps you in place
In the lonely, lonely space
Mercury, Venus, Earth and Mars
Are the first four among the stars
Pluto is the farthest among the sun
Everyone on Earth is having lots of fun
This poem is all about space
And planets orbiting at a pace.

Zakirah Girach (9)
Al-Ashraf Primary School, Gloucester

Shine Bright

Twinkle, twinkle, bright light shine,
my little star you are all but mine.

When I look at you my heart fills with joy,
to see you twinkle how splendid, oh what joy!

Twinkle, twinkle my little star shine,
all I want is for you to be mine.

Forever with me, for eternity.

Oh why, oh why, little bright light do you shine so far?
All I want is to touch your glow.

So bright, so white, so beautiful, so light.

My little bright light, oh my little bright light,
shine and glow, shine and glow.

Hasna Farooq (10)
Al-Ashraf Primary School, Gloucester

Why Don't You Go To Space?

Why don't you go to space
And earn your own place?
Don't just sit there, get a rocket
Which can at least
Fit into your pocket
Just go to space
And have an Olympic race
So for that you need your own pace
Just take space food
If you complain don't get into a mood
Go to Saturn
And just do a u-turn
Go to the moon
And play with the goon
Go to the Milky Way with lots of stars
And inside there is Mars
Go to Mars and see the volcano erupting
This is just exciting
Why don't you just go to space
And explore the galaxy which is full of chocolate
Why don't you go to Mercury
And make it your summer holiday?
Why don't you go to Neptune and just chill?
Why don't you go to space?

Umar Ahmed Ginwalla (9)
Al-Ashraf Primary School, Gloucester

Our Place Isn't Space

S pace is a place where no one lives
P eople and animals are nowhere to be seen
A ll you can see is galaxies
C old and lifeless the place sleeps
E arth is the place where I'd rather be.

Adil Desai (10)
Al-Ashraf Primary School, Gloucester

The Moon

Look here is the moon, the tale of my childhood
Hero of the Prince Epic
Hope of the mother
Here is the moon

Yes this is the moon
A land of my dreams
My mesmerising thought
A clear thought
With a blurred image

Here is the moon
My secret poetry
My miles away friend
I've got to be with the moon
I've just got to be
With the moon.

Umair Moosajee (10)
Al-Ashraf Primary School, Gloucester

Landing On The Moon

One, two, three . . . blast-off!
We are blasting off now.
In an hour and thirty minutes
We will have landed.
We love the moon
We love the moon
We really love the moon.
I can see the moon
I can see the moon
I can really see the moon.
Now we will land in three, two, one.
We have landed!
Now I want to go up again with my mum.

Shannon Willetts (9)
Ashwater Primary School, Beaworthy

A Poem In The Classic Style Of The Dark Ages 820 A.D.

Ivar throws his axe high into the air.
The sun reflects the light,
dazzling his men.
He catches the axe with skill beyond
the strength of normal men.
Ivar screams his battle cry
and his men echo the cry.
Courageously his men charge forward
upon the Saxon shield wall.
The two forces meet,
and the blood bath begins.
A crescendo of noise.
Men scream for their loved ones.
Bodies fall,
blood pours from deep gashes.
Skulls smash as axes fall.
Saxons flee in terror.
Saxons hewn down.
Victory for Ivar the Boneless.

Conall Cooban (9)
Ashwater Primary School, Beaworthy

Space Is Awesome

Where does it start?
Where does it end?
Aliens are not pretend.
There are masses of planets but they don't include Pluto.
It is hard for people to spot them.
Round and round the spacecraft travels, it might be bound to crash.
There are a lot of stars but they don't include Mars.
The spacecraft flies from dark to light.
The astronauts float inside the craft,
As it is also travelling through the light.

Ethan John Sweeney (9)
Ashwater Primary School, Beaworthy

Space Is Fun

Space is fun because all the planets are a dream.
Stars glitter in the sky.
Planets light up when astronauts fly up to space
To see . . .
The sun is a star.
Close to Earth is the moon.
A moon buggy I want to ride.
There is a planet called Pluto and another called Saturn.
Space is fun!

Keeley Cann (8)
Ashwater Primary School, Beaworthy

Up There

Up, up there in the air is an amazing world
With galaxies and stars like Jupiter and Mars.
Astronauts go to see that wonderful world
So why don't we?
Up, up there is an amazing light
That wonderful bright light guides you through the night.
Astronauts go to see that wonderful light
So why don't we?

Jasmine May Moon (10)
Ashwater Primary School, Beaworthy

Space Is Fun

Space is fun, you can see the aliens hiding.
Aliens are exciting, make great friends with them.
You can bounce up and down with them,
You can bounce up and down.
Float up into the sky and see Saturn, Mars and Earth.

Harvey Cann (7)
Ashwater Primary School, Beaworthy

O' Stars

Stars O' lovely stars,
How do you dance on the night air with nothing to stand on?

Stars O' beautiful stars,
How do you light up the universe with only the moon shining on you?

Stars O' pleasing stars,
How do you keep silent but watch over the world at sundown?

Stars, there is only one thing we know about you
Each dot of light in the sky represents a person that has passed
away in peace.

But now you are angels looking down from Heaven.

Rowan Tidball (9)
Ashwater Primary School, Beaworthy

Out Of This World

Some people are really lucky
Going up in a super-sized rocket,
Exploring the moon and seeing the view.
Planets and galaxies are amazing.
Incredible sights to see.
Places still to explore.
Space never stops growing.
Space races,
Flags on the moon.
Astronauts wearing kits.
Jumping up high.

Taylor Wood (8)
Ashwater Primary School, Beaworthy

Around Space

Space, space what a wonderful place,
With planets and discoveries.
Astronauts, astronauts from all over the world
Go to visit this amazing strange place.
Where the stars shine and the moon looks silvery grey,
People can visit it still to this day.
Rockets, rockets zooming speedily in the air
The great big noise gives people a scare.
Planets, planets still up there
Who knows what discoveries are still to share.
Planets like Uranus and Mars shine in the moonlight stars.

Isabella May Cummings (8)
Ashwater Primary School, Beaworthy

Supernova

Space is a place of prettiness,
It's a place of wonder,
Stars twinkling beautifully,
Bright shining stars stay all the time,
Gorgeous supernovas happening,
Big craters everywhere,
Moon dust in the air,
Lunar landings left behind, never to be seen again,
Moon buggies still where they were left,
Flags from previous people left
Where they put them back then.

Amy Erin Aisling Shirley (8)
Ashwater Primary School, Beaworthy

Moon's Light

M oon's light is colourful and dazzling
O n a frosty winter's night
O ne moon to shine above all
N othing gleams and shines more than this
S tars make a shiny mosaic in the dark sky

L ight like stars glow in the sky to guide the way
I n a supernova way a super power from Heaven
G lowing forever, mysteriously
H undreds of pulsating stars in the sky
T urning the world spinning around, night till day.

Isaac Joshua Renshaw (11)
Ashwater Primary School, Beaworthy

Outer Space

O uter space is the most amazing place,
U p there some sights you embrace,
T ake a look in the sky you will appreciate it,
E verybody will be awe-inspired,
R ight now look up there, throughout the galaxy,

S pace is awe-inspiring,
P eople look up there and think *what a place*
A nd there are masses of planets,
C ome on see it up there somewhere,
E ach person knows it, how about you?

Bethany Yelland (10)
Ashwater Primary School, Beaworthy

Up In Space

Once I travelled up in space
In my warm and colourful car
Silly me I forgot to tie my lace
My brand new shoe fell off on Mars
I tied my other lace up in space
An alien appeared with my other shoe covered with goo
I wiped my shoe off with my wipe
A rocket bashed in space and stars juggled in the sky
A special star came to the ground
The alien said, 'It's yours forever, it's a special space star.'

Harriet Moon (7)
Ashwater Primary School, Beaworthy

The Wonder Of Space

Where does space start and where does it end?
No one knows but there's more around each bend.
With so many galaxies, planets and stars
Our solar system has Uranus, Jupiter, Venus and Mars.
Also in our Milky Way is Earth, that's us
With Neptune, Mercury and Saturn
We orbit the sun, if we get any closer we might even burn.
The universe seems to go on forever and ever.
Whoever made it was really very clever.

Julia Parrin (8)
Ashwater Primary School, Beaworthy

Space Poem

Space, space oh big dark place,
Stars, stars oh beautiful stars,
Moon how do you light up the sky at night?
Moon you look so close but you're so far away,
There are still millions of secrets to be discovered.
Giant planets big, bright and bold.
Stars travelling towards Mars,
Aliens floating in the vast dark space.
Can we recognise their strange face?

Harry Ayre (9)
Ashwater Primary School, Beaworthy

10, 9, 8, 7, 6, 5, 4, 3, 2, 1, Blast-Off!

10, 9, 8, 7, 6, 5, 4, 3, 2, 1 off we go
We are not going slow . . . fast, faster through the Milky Way fast,
Faster through the constellation of the ball.
Now we are going slower and slower, oh no fuel, we have run out of fuel.
Oh dear we can't get to Pluto, but I was looking forward to that.
It looks like we are stuck.
We are going to get out, come what may
I doubt that.

McKenzie John Sweeney (8)
Ashwater Primary School, Beaworthy

Space

Saturn is bright gold and Jupiter is bold.
Flying saucers up in space,
When they fly past they fly with grace.
I dream of flying up to Mars,
Whizzing by like a shooting star.
Tiny little stars are floating past
Great, big, giant Mars.
Neptune, Neptune so blue and bright,
I would like to wish on a star tonight.

Rosie Seymour (9)
Ashwater Primary School, Beaworthy

Up In Space

The moon is a planet that people want to see.
The moon is a space where people want to be.
I see the planets gazing down on me
and when I look at them they smile at me.
The stars are bright, yellow and light,
They are beautiful in the darkness of night.
Space is a place where people want to go,
Will they like it?
I don't know!

Lily Horsburgh (9)
Ashwater Primary School, Beaworthy

Meteorites

Meteorites crashing into rocks
Meteorites coming closer to Earth every second
The sun burning hotter and hotter
The universe will soon die . . .

Harvey Moon (9)
Ashwater Primary School, Beaworthy

An Alien Invasion

They pummelled through our defence
As the war of the worlds got more intense
Gunshots, rockets and lasers being shot
Dead bodies on the ground left there to rot
The ultimatum was not succeeded
More ammo and food was surely needed.

We evacuated to the moon
As we knew the creatures would be here soon
We knew they were coming, we knew they'd hunt us down
I looked at everyone's faces and they all had a frown
But I had to do something, I had to survive
I had to find food, I had to stay alive.

With aliens around I can't get to sleep
I hear the phones ringing *beep, beep!*
But we couldn't pick them up or we'd be compromised
And the least that would happen is being pulverised
We need to set up camp, we need to set up base
We need to kill those things, we need to win the race.

Those creatures are misanthropes
All we have left is hope
Their ships have a force field
They were so big, it was impossible for humans to build
No one can believe this
Goodbye Earth, you will be missed.

Ewan Millard (10)
Bugle School, St. Austell

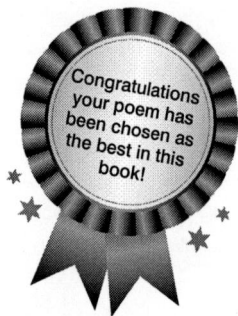

Congratulations your poem has been chosen as the best in this book!

Outer Space Mysteries

O rbiting an undiscovered galaxy,
U ltimate exploration if we come across extra-
T errestrial life
E verybody wants to know what is out in that amplitude
R eceiving unknown radio signals, could there really be alien life out
there?

S upernatural black holes
P iercing apart universes
A s they are pulled into the vacuum within
C ertified for exploration of these unpolished specimens
E cstatic energy formed by pulverised universes

M anifesting oxygen loss
Y ou are searching for the airlock
S ilent pressure, crushing your spacecraft like a tin can
T elling Houston, 'We might not make it back'
E verything you have found, sent back to them
R ed lights flashing all around
I nterlocking screws and bolts torn apart
E mpress of space, the sun
S tares at me as my life ebbs away.

Elliot Batten (11)
Bugle School, St. Austell

Out At Space

As cold as ice
As bitter as snow
Unknown territory out there . . .
It's as murky as the dark side of the moon
Aliens roaming the holes
Stars hovering over the light
Alien camps ahead
Goodbye aliens I'm going home!

Logan Exell (11)
Bugle School, St. Austell

Unmarked Territory

U niverse Anonymous, that's what it should be called
N ASA unexplored but don't be fooled
M achines aren't that good because they can be ruled
A lways on wheels, some just record sound
R ed planet's too hot so it's never been fully found
K eeping safe in space is very hard
E ven when you're feeling lonely you don't want a card
D inosaurs, Daleks the truth could unfold

T errible tales have been told
E xterminate, the Daleks say but up here they'll be blown away
R eal life
R eal space when you're up here time goes with no pace
I s it real? It can't be real
T he general public have no idea how I feel
O rbiting that's what the moon does to us
R eally no trouble, don't make a fuss
Y oda gave me the force to do this poem!

Tye Thompson Sammut (10)
Bugle School, St. Austell

Outer Space

O ut and around exploring!
U nder gravity
T he sun beaming like a volcano
E arth spinning, spinning
R aging, how do I work all these crazy buttons?

S peaking to my mate saying how brilliant this is!
P luto, it's only a small planet
A liens? Have not seen them yet but I'm hopeful I will
C an't even see the fluffy
E arth, is mighty and high!

Lauren Webber (11)
Bugle School, St. Austell

Spectacular Space

As the planets flow
The moon glows
Bright in the sky
Stars shine.

As the moon's gravity pulls us in
You can look deep within
Satellites, stars, space stations and stones
All make the solar system flow.

Pretty things, purple things and pink things glow
Aliens shouting, 'Go, go, go!'
Beep, boop, beep!
NASA's calling, time to go!

Paige Buckland (10)
Bugle School, St. Austell

The Search For Aliens

O rbiting in a mysterious world
U nderneath or above us is something
T he robots collecting samples
E xtraterrestrials roaming in another world
R ockets searching for alien life

S earching for them or they are searching for us?
P eople scared of an alien invasion
A re we going to be abducted? Or are we going to shoot down
    UFOs?
C old ice planets or jelly planets?
E xtraterrestrials wiping out Earth?

Adam MacInally (10)
Bugle School, St. Austell

The Amazing Outer Space

O rbiting around a mysterious galaxy
U ranus is circled by a number of rings
T he sun shines bright in the sky
E normous planets floating around space
R ockets zooming around the planets

S aturn's rings are a brilliant sight
P lanet Earth is a luminous light
A liens flying in their UFOs
C omets made all of the dinosaurs extinct
E vil aliens approaching!

Charlie Murray (10)
Bugle School, St. Austell

Outer Space

O rbiting around a mysterious galaxy
U nknown territory above us!
T he sun circling down on Earth
E arthlings, that's what aliens say
R ockets blasting to space

S atellites orbiting the Earth
P luto shouting
A liens invading
C ombining rockets
E arth is being invaded.

Joshua Downes Combellack (11)
Bugle School, St. Austell

Outer Space

O rbiting around a mysterious galaxy
U nknown territory lurking near
T he moon getting smaller and smaller
E xtraterrestrial planet encountering!
R ocket out of fuel!

S tars around
P lanets nowhere
A liens circling me
C aptured
E ek!

TJ Colvin (10)
Bugle School, St. Austell

Outer Space

O ver the moon going in semi-circles
U nder Mars
T he sun shining bright
E xtraterrestrials watching us!
R ockets are going to space

S pace
P eople on Earth, aliens are coming!
A ntique buttons in the rockets
C ans of oil have been used in rockets
E mergency, aliens, Mars is getting attacked!

Ethan Lee (10)
Bugle School, St. Austell

The Space Giant

The giant
Lifts his hand up high
Touching the Earth
He cushions it gently in his palm
His friends do the same
But to the moon and sun
The stars up high
Lights up the sky making it navy blue
His friend slowly spins the sun around the Earth
His other friend does the same
But with the moon
Slowly space starts to form
All the other planets that we know today
Then slowly the giant spins the planet
Like a football on his fingers

And that's how our planet, moon and sun move.

Freya Pegley (10)
Christow Community School, Exeter

Up High

The sky is a swishing sequined cloak
That covers the world in a thick, black smoke.

The black hole gurgles as he eats his meal
Turning and churning like a fast moving wheel.

The sun tries to shine bright
Desperate for it to be light.

Under the moon's careful eye
Earth lets out a contented sigh.
In the distance a rocket jets up high
I ask myself why go up there, why?

Then suddenly I see a comet come out of the gloom
And I know for this Earth it is certain doom!

Emma Gervers (11)
Christow Community School, Exeter

The Hole In Space

A colourful mist
Fills the sky
A dark, swirly dish
Way up high
It draws you in
It sucks you up
I'm as small as a pin,
I'm a baby pup.
Speechless at its beauty
The spell it casts me under
It's pretty or it's brutal
Is he nice? I ponder
His glow's so enchanting
I sometimes hear him groan
For he's a black hole
So alone . . .

Rhiannon Corbett (10)
Christow Community School, Exeter

Planets

Mercury, closest to the sun, hottest, closest number one.
Venus, pretty fun. Even so I weigh a ton.
Earth, the home of all, although I'm really rather small.
Mars, I sizzle as I burn your feet, if people come to visit me I will greet.
Jupiter, the gods of all gods, most of my servants do the jobs.
Saturn, I'm bling with all my jewellery and my rings.
Uranus, some think may be a little rude, but if they do I'll be in a mood.
Neptune, the king of the sea, even though he's a lot bigger than me
Pluto, he's the baby, I want to play with him maybe, just maybe.
So there you have it, all the planets. Oh, did I mention there's one called Janet?

Leela Gibson (9)
Christow Community School, Exeter

The Dark Side Of The Moon

The light to the dark
The clear to the mist
The kiss that will freeze you suddenly
The dream to the nightmare
The happy to the dull
The pitch-black doom haunts your heart
The blanket of cold, the blaze of sun
You stay still as a statue
The dark side of the moon.

Verity Bushell (11)
Christow Community School, Exeter

Losing Control

A blue haze surrounds us
A sleepy feeling arises
Everything stops
Then *jolt* . . .
Smoke rises
Shadows darting
Engines failing
Losing control.

Katie Rebecca Tose (11)
Christow Community School, Exeter

What Am I?

Looming around the galaxy
Hovering majestically above
Glittering contentedly like a proud and shining bug!
I'm all around, flooding the sky
I flicker sometimes when the dazzling sun is in my eyes
I dance, I fly, I float around up high . . .
What am I?

Rebecca Freshney-Lee (11)
Christow Community School, Exeter

Space

S is for the twinkling stars that light up the night
P is for Pluto the little planetarium rock
A is for aliens of all bright coloured spots, shapes and sizes
C is for clusters of stars up in the dark sky
E is for the excited emotion of an astronaut.

Grace Hoskin (9)
Christow Community School, Exeter

Who Am I?

My sparkling stars glisten in the damp, dark sky
In a spacecraft you'll be able to fly!
My asteroids are falling down like crashing plumes of ash
They come tumbling down in a crackling flash
I live far, far away in a gloomy galaxy
Up here you cannot drive a taxi!
Saturn is famous for its curly rings
This planet is just like a majestic king!
My Milky Way is a dim glowing band
And some of my planets are made out of silky sand.
Venus is pretty, pink and is extremely cold,
People like to discover this and become totally bold!
My sun is an ordinary, fixed shining star
From down here it is fantastically far
Jupiter has a great red spot
But you cannot see the amazing dot!
The Earth's moon doesn't produce its own light
Imagine if you saw it, it would be a tremendous sight!
My Earth is the third planet from the sun
Also my awesome Earth weighs a ton!
Mercury, Uranus, Pluto and Mars
These line up with my shimmering stars
I am a gigantic place
My name is . . . *outer space!*

Holly Iona Jenkin (8)
Connor Downs Primary School, Hayle

Spooky Space

The sun is a golden ball
High up in the sky

'Til the magnificent moon
Dances slowly and passes her by

It is then night – dark as coal
But somehow magical

Planets shine like diamonds
Still and beautiful

The asteroids circle the sun
Some big and some small

'Where will we go next?' they cry
'Will we stay or fall?'

The galaxy is glowing like the coal of a fire
Whose flames go up, reaching higher and higher

Our Milky Way is a fantastic place
As strange and colourful as a clown's face.

Lewis Mitchelmore (9)
Connor Downs Primary School, Hayle

Space

Swirling
The planets prancing around like ballerinas
Stars out at night
You only see them if they twinkle bright
The Milky Way is a bunch of stars
And there's also a chocolate bar
Does it taste like Mars?
People say the moon tastes like cheese
Dose it really taste of peas?
Glittering
The stars shining like diamonds.

Libby Roberts (9)
Connor Downs Primary School, Hayle

Out Of This World!

Out in space there are extraordinary things to be discovered
Uranus is a tilted planet which rotates on its side
The furthest planet from the flaming hot sun is Neptune, the slowest
planet

Orbiting Neptune are fourteen moons
Forever to be remembered
To be explored many times
Halley's Comet is the most famous and can only be seen every
seventy-seven years

Isolated from other planets is the dwarf planet Pluto
Saturn is named after the Roman god Saturnus
Whole wide galaxy to be discovered

Outstanding Milky Way
Round and round planets orbit
Life is impossible in space
Dreams can come true if you want to go to the moon!

Madison Newton (8)
Connor Downs Primary School, Hayle

Super Space!

Space is a place
Where asteroids fly and aliens pace
Past all the sparkling stars
Who knows if there's life on Mars?

Astronauts fly up in rockets
Aliens pace
But stars come shooting down
Rocks fly through our system and then they come back down

Have you been to space?
Do you know what it's like?
You don't really need to pack a case
Unless you are called Mike.

Chloe Brown (8)
Connor Downs Primary School, Hayle

Sensational Space

S aturn's huge rings are awesome
E arth is amusing
N eptune is as blue as the lovely sea
S parkling like a shining star in the morning
A steroids float randomly
T ouring around the burning sun
I wish I could go with them
O n a journey that's lots of fun
N othing is more beautiful than space
A ll the people would agree
L eaving here to be up there

S urely space is the best place to be
P luto is so far
A way
C an't even get there in my lifetime!
E very night I look up into space.

Maya Dennis (8)
Connor Downs Primary School, Hayle

Spectacular Space

I look up from Earth and try to see
The wonderful planets looking at me

The spectacular stars
Close to Neptune, Jupiter and Mars

Always I look up high
Looking for planets in the sky

I think my favourite is Neptune
Oh . . . and the moon.

I think they are the best
Out of all the rest.

Paige Collinge (10)
Connor Downs Primary School, Hayle

The Ocean Of Black

As I look up into the starlit sky,
I see a flaming comet whisking by.
Silence is happening all around,
The atmosphere doesn't make a single sound.
I can see the Northern hemisphere,
It's amazing, I'm beyond Earth up here!
The moon is making a luminous glow,
Three thousand stars surround it, or so I know.
The Milky Way, a group of stars in space,
I can see the Milky Way from this particular place.
Neptune is as cold as cold can be,
A beautiful colour though, the colour of the sea.
I look down at Earth, long to go back,
Down to the beach and out of the black.

Hannah Seaton (9)
Connor Downs Primary School, Hayle

Astonishing Space

Shooting stars whizzing through the jet-black sky,
Some nights they don't appear, they might be a bit shy.
Planets orbiting the bright, shimmering sun,
Spinning round one by one.
People have been to space,
I really would love to go there because it looks ace.

Asteroids shoot through the deep dark galaxy
Hitting anything in its gloomy way.
Comets zooming through the atmosphere
Looking like fireworks on bonfire night.
Earth looks like a speck from outer space
But I live there and it's a really big place.

Harry Charman (8)
Connor Downs Primary School, Hayle

Out Of This World

With my telescope I can reach the stars,
I can swim in the seas on the surface of the moon,
And see the burning glow of Mars.
A comet leaves a blurry scar across the outer space,
Will it ever reach a destination in another time or place?
I long to be an astronaut, in my rocket flying over
Satellites and planets, towards a . . . *supernova!*
Passing through the Milky Way to another universe
Exploring every corner to find another Earth
I finally reach a space station, orbiting the moon
The journey has been amazing, but I'd like to go home soon!

Erin Freestone (8)
Connor Downs Primary School, Hayle

Space

S pace is spectacular
P lanets are phenomenal
A mazing asteroids
C racking comets
E xtraordinary Earth

I ncredible impact
S mashing solar system

A stonishing atmosphere
C reative cheese. The substance that the moon is made of
E arth is where we live!

Caleb Harris (9)
Connor Downs Primary School, Hayle

Space

In a galaxy far away where the stars glitter and glowing asteroids storm past!
When you land there's probably aliens waiting to eat you!
And a few seconds later all you can hear is crunching and munching.
Then a voice comes in and says, 'Mmm you're tasty!'

Suddenly a star explodes with purples and reds with all the rest of the rainbow.
Then a bunch goes off like fireworks.
When dark comes it comes quick.
Half a minute it's . . . pitch-black.

Jacob Sandow (10)
Connor Downs Primary School, Hayle

Sensational Space

S ensational space is henceforth amazing, it will blow your eyes out of their sockets
P erfect planets always orbit the roasting sun but they move slower than a snail in a Derby race
A mazing stars glistening in the jet sky where there is no oxygen and also no gravity
C rystal clear sky where aliens boogie and have a midnight disco (that sounds fun)
E xcellent sun keeps Earth alive and even the coldest most freezing planets alive.

Matthew Bonds (9)
Connor Downs Primary School, Hayle

Space – A Wonderful Place

Out in space
A dark and gloomy place

It's magical
Earth shaped like a football

Shining stars
Make you go, 'Ah!'

All over the place
They are amazing and ace.

Jess Caves (9)
Connor Downs Primary School, Hayle

Outside Of Planet Earth

Space is ace
Everyone loves the glistening stars of outer space
Everyone loves the mesmerising, spectacular colours of outer space
Pinks, blues and purples are the amazing colours of outer space
Mercury, Venus and our special Earth
Are closest to the sizzling sun of outer space
Saturn, Uranus and Neptune are the furthest planets of outer space
The asteroid belt is between Mars and Jupiter of outer space
Swirling, twirling shooting stars are in the darkness of outer space.

Harrison John Rice (8)
Connor Downs Primary School, Hayle

Space

Earth is such a wonderful place, but I wonder what it's like in outer space?
Are we alone or are there others light years from home?
There is no planet redder than Mars and thousands of dancing, twinkling stars.
The sun and moon make day and night, space is such a wonderful sight!
Earth is such a wonderful place but I wonder what it's like in *outer space?*

Darren Vann (9)
Connor Downs Primary School, Hayle

Fantastic Space

In space there are phenomenal stars
Fiery extreme asteroids
The Milky Way is a brilliant home
And as perfect as a gooey chocolate bar
Spinning planets in a flabbergasting galaxy
The emerald Earth glittering like a beautiful, shining green diamond
Epic spaceships swooping around, zooming past planets
Like an extremely cool bullet from a perfect gun.

Jake Mellor (9)
Connor Downs Primary School, Hayle

Space

S pace is cool, space is magical, spectacular space
P ast the moon, past Rome and past all my friends at home
A stronauts floating through the universe. Passing all the planets
C elebrating when they get back from dark and gloomy space
E xisting in space, what a trip space is, as dark as when the electric
  goes off.

Abbie Collinge (10)
Connor Downs Primary School, Hayle

Phenomenal Space

S ensational, spectacular space is surrounded by perfect planets in
  our solar system
P henomenal planets with their moons taking trips around the
  flaming sun
A mazing comets soaring through the awesome atmosphere
C rackling asteroids burn up in the protective ozone layer
E arth, the only known planet with life living around it, thanks to the
  sun, the basis for human life.

Tom James (8)
Connor Downs Primary School, Hayle

Out Of Space

I can see the crumbling comets whiz by
The Earth looks really small I'm up so high
The deep dark black sky
And then a rocket comes zooming by
The galaxy around us, the Milky Way
Filled with a billion stars, or so they say
I look down at Earth, long to go back
Home looks so small in the sea of black.

Eve Penhaligon (8)
Connor Downs Primary School, Hayle

Up To The Moon

Rocket at the ready to fly all the way to the moon,
The astronauts will be there very soon!
Soaring high up, up they go,
See the Earth all miniature down below!
Up through the stars, zooming past Mars,
Soon they will land on the moon's hard bumpy ground!
You never know who you might meet,
A little green man with a head like a sheep.

Ethan Hancock (10)
Connor Downs Primary School, Hayle

Fabulous Looking Space

S hiny stars in the night sky
P luto is a very small and cold planet
A steroids zooming around the belt between Mars and Jupiter
C rashing down to Earth
E xcited children looking through a big telescope at all the
marvellous planets.

Sapphire Newton (9)
Connor Downs Primary School, Hayle

Sensational Space

Space is epic, you have to go there
Milky Way is the best there you can see
Stars glisten in the dark night
You can't live till you go to space, so go, go, go . . .
Pluto is white as snow and Uranus is blue, hurry, hurry.

Alfie Spencer- Amos (8)
Connor Downs Primary School, Hayle

Space

S pace is extraordinary
P lanets orbiting around the sun
A stonishing asteroids, shooting through the atmosphere
C ool in every way
E verlasting, never to end.

Dylan Thomas (9)
Connor Downs Primary School, Hayle

Space And Extras!

Stars dazzling
Planet sightings
Rockets zooming
Planet findings

Comets soaring
Spacemen flying
Planets racing
Sun is floating

Wondrous galaxies
Speed of light
Monkey testing
Stars are shining very bright

Milky Way big and swirling
Asteroid belt staying still
Moon sprinting like Usain Bolt
Sun burning bright day and night

Ellie Dash (11)
Heamoor Community Primary School, Penzance

Running Out Of Time . . .

S ometimes I look in my rocket
P eace up in the stars
A t night I think about it
C an I go to Mars?
E verything around is making me cough

I 'm running out of breath
S oon I will drop!

C reepy pictures fill my head
O utside my head I see light
O h it's only a dream
L ike . . . is that right?

Daisy Perry (9)
Heamoor Community Primary School, Penzance

A Brief Journey

As I take a glance at space
To endeavour in oblivion
I encounter a rogue imagination
I mourn the lost souls of gargantuan gold mines
And stalk the mazes of eternal bliss
The universe is fluent in wonder
Nevermore, I see the garden of creation
For time shall pass, thus civilisation ceases
Death becomes of me, if in my brief odyssey
I shall never return . . .

Wilbur Slade (10)
Heamoor Community Primary School, Penzance

Space

The moon is as big as a boulder
Sailing through the sky
Whizzing rockets in outer space
Flying very high.

Stars glittering
Lighting up the night
They glitter when you're sleeping
Tucked in bed, very tight.

Mars is as hot as an oven
It is fiery red
I saw a meteorite fly through the sky
It whistled as it sped.

When you look up into the sky at night
You will find these things
This is just a taster
Of what space brings.

Charlie Edwards (10)
Heamoor Community Primary School, Penzance

In The Night Sky

As I looked up to the sky
It was the middle of night
I stood gazing on the damp lawn
Whilst my family were tucked up tight.

The sky was full of stars
But then a comet sped past
I jumped from foot to foot
I wish this feeling would last.

Ismay Shannon Cornish-Murphy (11)
Heamoor Community Primary School, Penzance

Lifeless

L iving creatures No.1
I mprisonment of aliens down black holes
F ire flying sun spitting balls of fire
E clipse lowering near to Earth
L eaning planets posing towards gravity
E ffortless gravity, objects floating into nothingness
S pacecraft landing on the moon, dust everywhere
S hocking shocks landing everywhere, big balls of fire up ahead.

Jaime-Lei Holland (10)
Heamoor Community Primary School, Penzance

Alien

A mplified ship
L oving
I nspiring to write
E nding never habitat
N ever anything really there.

Myrtle Amelie Ratcliffe (10)
Heamoor Community Primary School, Penzance

Space

S ailing rockets
P lanets everywhere
A liens, aliens
C omets coming
E arth behind us.

Chloe Leonard (9)
Heamoor Community Primary School, Penzance

The Aliens

S pace is huge
P lanets can be big and small
A liens come from big alien ships
C omets flying side to side
E veryone comes home.

Thomas Tregarthen (10)
Heamoor Community Primary School, Penzance

To The Moon

S uper star shooter
T o the moon we shall go
A liens live here
R unning around everywhere we go.

Skye Marie Parsons (10)
Heamoor Community Primary School, Penzance

Space Life

I'm a magic alien
Space is my home
Watch out for the black hole
Technology is all around.

Ruth Ireland (11)
Heamoor Community Primary School, Penzance

Wonders – Haiku

Space is wonderful
It is a wonderful sight
Space is our shield.

Chloe Patrisha Bugden (10)
Heamoor Community Primary School, Penzance

Space Times – Haiku

I love space rockets
I have a space dog called Tim
My son is with me.

Mollie Maycock (10)
Heamoor Community Primary School, Penzance

We Are Best Friends

B efore I met you
E verything was dark
S hooting everywhere like a star
T ill you are tired

F riends forever
R est while you can
I will stay with you
E nd will not come
N ever stop believing
D estined for things to go well for us.

You are my best friend and always will be.

Libby Wright (10)
Leigham Primary School, Plymouth

On Mars!

On Mars there is,
Mars, Mars, Milky Way bars,
I can see Jupiter, I can see Mars,
Also eatable stars,
Spinning planets around the cars,
All I can see in the night sky
Is planets, stars and galaxies.

Abigail Louise Liddington
Mithian School, St. Agnes

Planets And Stars

Stars, stars, planets and stars
I can see Jupiter, I can see Mars
Stars, stars planets and stars
I can see Milky Way bars
Stars, stars, planets and stars
I can see different colour stars.

Abbie McIndoe (9)
Mithian School, St. Agnes

Mars Bars

Mars, Milky Way bars
Creamy chocolate stars
I can see Jupiter, I can see Mars
Jupiter has got a jelly and even some wellies
But Mars has neither.

Isabella Manley (9)
Mithian School, St. Agnes

Stars Are Like Snowflakes

Stars are like snowflakes,
Scattered 'cross the sky.
Stars are like snowflakes,
Dancing up so high.

Stars are like snowflakes,
Hope in the black of night.
Stars are like snowflakes,
Melting in the light.

May Robinson (11)
Mrs Ethelston's CE (VA) Primary School, Lyme Regis

The Circle Invasion

Oh no! The aliens are here
They all have a giant gun!
They come with massive armies
They won't stop till they are done

They come as fast as a race car
They are so very strong
Their eyes are bloodshot red
And they really rather pong

Boom! Crash! Bang! The aliens are shooting
Just like a fire-breathing dragon
They're in the shape of a circle
I could not use my tongue

Why do they come?
We really do not know
They probably like it
Their leader's name is Po

If you see them
You have to run
You have to escape
And it is not fun

The aliens have hidden
So now we eat a pear
We still look for them
But we know they are there

The aliens are leaving
They're going to Mars
The aliens are scared
They leave on the stars.

Ethan Clark (8)
Offa's Mead Academy, Chepstow

Bizarre Aliens!

As I looked up high into the dark night sky,
A spaceship came into sight,
A weird looking creature waved madly at me,
In fact it gave me a fright!

It landed like a shooting star,
Flying through the sky,
It ran around the universe,
And landed with a cry!

Its hands were green and gloopy,
Its head was rather fat,
I wouldn't like to be it,
But I would rather be a cat!

Its blood was cranberry juice,
Its eyes were made of clocks,
Its breath smells like dirty socks,
And its legs are made of blocks!

And if you want to see these,
Bizarre, disgusting beings,
You'll find them doing a weird thing,
And it is called peeing!

Grace Utovou (9)
Offa's Mead Academy, Chepstow

Super Stars

S hiny, shimmering stars igniting the sky.
T antalising, terrific, phenomenal planets glow like multiple glow worms.
A liens live on both Earth and Mars.
R ockets rapidly racing, trying to land on Venus.
S uper spacemen surfing dreamily around the rings of Saturn.

Tiana Dutson
Offa's Mead Academy, Chepstow

Awful Aliens

The aliens are invading,
It's disturbing but it's true,
Who knows what they want,
We don't have a clue.

They crashed like a boulder,
Covered in fuel and steam,
Then out they flew all black and blue,
They came in several teams.

Their hands are mossy twigs,
Their heads are weird machines,
Their bodies are just like spuds,
Their legs are runner beans.

Their blood is greasy goo,
Their eyes are made of salt,
Their hair is spaghetti hoops,
Their feet are just like vaults.

Also, if you want to meet these
Unmannerly ants,
You will find them hiding in your house,
Because they will be hiding in your pants.

Harry Dymock (10)
Offa's Mead Academy, Chepstow

Space

S hooting, shiny, shimmering stars igniting the night sky
P luto prancing and dancing, orbiting the sun
A mazing rockets racing rapidly like bullets from a gun
C ool comets crashing and cascading into the enormous Earth
E xtremely terrifying, gruesome aliens attacking Pluto.

Darcy Wheeler (8)
Offa's Mead Academy, Chepstow

Alien Invasion

Do not disturb the aliens
Who have just arrived from space
They travelled through the Milky Way
From a great enormous place!

They landed with a *clash . . . bang . . . boom . . . !*
Before my very eyes
But when they pranced out of their ship
They looked up to the skies.

Green as mushy peas they looked
They smell like stinky socks
Eyes as black as a cat
My body was in shock!

Despite their look, so mean
They tried to be my friend
They wrapped their arms around me
We were best friends in the end.

Niamh White (8)
Offa's Mead Academy, Chepstow

Planet Pluto

Forgotten planet
Tiny dwarf
Shimmering sparkling
Left alone
Let down
Hard rock
No human beings
Terribly misunderstood

Can you guess who this planet is . . .
It is Planet Pluto!

Sophie Woodall (10)
Offa's Mead Academy, Chepstow

Astonishing Aliens

As I looked high into the black blanket sky,
Aliens were flying like a mental meteorite!
On their astonishing saucers they zoomed around space,
Bang! Boom! Crash! They landed under the magical moonlight.

Their hands are great, greasy tentacles,
Their heads are insane machines.
Their bodies are wiggly worms,
And they smell like gone off sardines!

Their blood is thick with helium,
Their eyes are green grenades!
Their breath smells like rotten eggs,
I wonder if they have hearing aids?

I wouldn't like to see these,
Courageous, unattractive, rank beings.
Unfortunately they're working near my street,
I was hoping they'd be great play things!

Levi Robinson
Offa's Mead Academy, Chepstow

Space

S tars glowing in the night sky like glow worms
P lanets in the night sky reflecting off the moon
A liens live on Earth, Mars and Saturn
C ould you see the Planet Mars all the way from Earth?
E ver fancied an adventure going into space?

Elizabeth Monk
Offa's Mead Academy, Chepstow

Alien Attack

The aliens are coming,
It's frightening but it's true,
Even though they're friendly,
And look kind of blue.

They came in like a meteor,
With the power to make us beg,
Whilst some of them are resting,
And calling us a rotten egg.

All of them are now leaving,
And screaming all about,
The superhero Mario,
Swinging a poisonous trout.

Finally we are all free,
Those aliens have fleed,
Now we can do what we want,
This is why you have now sat down to read.

Lucas Hayes (10)
Offa's Mead Academy, Chepstow

Dragons

D ragons breathe out red-hot fire.
R un higher ice dragon!
A dragon has ginormous sharp teeth.
G reat dragons are nasty and eat beef.
O n top of a tall, dark mountain some flowery dragons live.
N ot very well dragons can't breathe out flamey, hot fire.
S ome dragons have slithery tails.

Imogen Mia Turnbull (8)
Parkham Primary School, Bideford

Dragons

D ragons breathe red-hot fire and one's a big liar.
R ough dragon as tall as a skyscraper.
A lmost stronger than a big, bad, red dragon.
G reen dragon as bright as a shiny star.
O nce a year he eats and beats.
N aughty dragon, his name is Flame.
S cary days are where the small people run away.

Jonathan Lang (7)
Parkham Primary School, Bideford

Journey Through Space

Stars twinkle in space,
They twinkle in the blackness,
Beaming out their light.

They twinkle next to,
The neighbouring planets,
That spin round and round.

Jupiter and Mars,
Are both near to the surface,
Of the human world.

Earth is where humans,
Live and build their small brick homes,
And sleep at night-time.

The hot, blazing sun,
Keeps us from the chilly cold,
And gives us some light.

The Earth sends people,
Up to the white, rocky moon,
To be world heroes.

The hard meteors,
Soar through the blackness of space,
And get faster and faster.

Matthew Oliver (10)
Redhills Community Primary School, Exeter

Taking Off

I saw a shuttle,
Feeling as cold as Arctic ice.
My heart, as cold as the night sky,
They had finished fuelling the bomb-like tank,
Into the cockpit, I emerged up the steps slowly,
'Ten,' said mission control. 'Nine.' Take-off was coming quicker,
After all these years I was finally ready to go up to the seas of black,
'Eight.' Waving to my astronaut friends out the small, dusty window,
'Six, five.' Sitting on the grenade-like shuttle,
'Three, two, one.' All the smoke in the air,
'Zero, blast-off!' We shot into the air like a cheetah,
Fire, smoke and pieces of the shuttle blew away,
We were there, wow! It was so beautiful,
The moon was as big as a gigantic satellite.
I asked to land, 'Yes, you can.'
But where were the stars, it was pitch-black,
The buggy came out, we grabbed some moon rock,
Eventually we had to start coming down,
To unbeautiful Earth.
Soon I will be back,
In about a year or two.
He has one last glimpse at the black ocean, we shoot back down,
A parachute appears,
We are here,
Welcome home to you all,
Hello everyone,
I am home.

Harvey Smith (10)
Redhills Community Primary School, Exeter

Space

I am walking up the steps.
About to set foot in a 100 ton black, white and gold bomb.
My eyes are like saucepans.
When I get up there, will I die?
Our mission, to land on the moon.
Gather rocks, stay up there for two days and dock with ISS.
What could go wrong? Everything!
Then the countdown.
10 . . . I'm terrified . . .
9 . . . I'm ecstatic . . .
8 . . . I'm animated . . .
7 . . . My head has shrunk into my shoulders . . .
6 . . . Will I die? . . .
5 . . . The seat belt's too tight . . .
4 . . . Not long now . . .
3 . . . Inside I'm screaming like a girl . . .
2 . . . Hurry up time! . . .
1 . . . This is it! . . .
Blast-off! The engines roar like a lion.
The engines are screaming.
Ten minutes later I'm floating.
Then we land on the moon.
I stuff my hands with rocks then take them back.
It is impossible to sleep from the *hmmmm* of the spaceship.
We dock with ISS.
Then we meet our families.

Jack Kingdom (10)
Redhills Community Primary School, Exeter

Space

I looked up at space,
The world is spinning I thought,
The world is called Earth.

I looked up again,
And there were lots of shiny stars,
And then I dreamed of . . .

Would space wear something?
A cloak with shiny buttons,
And colourful ones!

Would space sing something?
A song that was very quiet,
Or was very loud.

What else would space be?
Maybe a big elephant,
That walked on and on.

Would space eat something?
Maybe the rockets that come,
He swallows them whole.

Emily George (11)
Redhills Community Primary School, Exeter

Outer Space

O ceans of black.
U nknown until now.
T he things inside the rocket floating about.
E verywhere there are sparkling stars.
R ight away from family.

S eeing the huge Earth far below.
P lanets drifting around.
A nnouncing things to the space station.
C an't hear anything outside.
E ating mostly dry foods.

Ruben Isaac Northcott
Redhills Community Primary School, Exeter

Journey To Space

Space is so endless.
There are aliens in space.
Aliens are true.

Space has many stars.
The stars sparkle in the night.
Stars look small but big.

People say that the
Meteors are so deadly.
They are very big!

People have been in space.
They rode rockets to space.
They felt amazing!

Space is amazing.
Space is very dark,
But the sun is bright.

The moon is so white.
The moon is very empty.
Aliens on the moon.

Alex Dumitru (10)
Redhills Community Primary School, Exeter

Space, The Universe Above

The universe above holds many mysteries,
Many untold secret tales.
So many people want to know them,
But no one will say a word.
What if there are aliens?
Living above our heads!
What if our lost items,
Are floating by themselves?
This is only what could be happening,
Miles above our heads.

Amy Bristow (11)
Redhills Community Primary School, Exeter

Space Poem

When we go to space,
it's like sitting on an
exploding bomb about
to explode,
I feel so alive,
I feel so nervous when
we get going,
I feel as nervous as
when I started school.
Space is as dark as
night.
Stars are like
diamonds in the sky.
Planets are gigantic
rocks in space.
When we go back to
Earth the spaceship
feels sad.
Bang! goes the crash
landing.

Marlie Louise Vittles (9)
Redhills Community Primary School, Exeter

Space

Space wore a black coat,
It was dark as a shadow,
White spots were on it.

Space invented time,
It is an infinite place,
Space is unexplored.

It's lonely in space,
But aliens might be there,
They might be on Mars.

Leo Brooklyn Gliddon (10)
Redhills Community Primary School, Exeter

Space!

What could space be like?
Could it be a big, black cape,
Or a lovely, bright song.

Maybe it's a race,
Or it's covered in a cape,
But empty like a crate.

There are silver, shining stars,
And anxious aliens too!
The stars shining too.

The rocket slicing,
Through planets like a big knife,
And lands on the moon.

The planets are big,
But some planets are very small,
Saturn has a ring.

Is this what space is like?
What do you think?

Brett Woodland (10)
Redhills Community Primary School, Exeter

Space – Haiku

The best astronaut!
The astronaut went to space.
He said amazing.

He stopped at the moon,
To look at the view, no way.
Space is a big coat.

Space keeps going on
And on and on still going.
It still keeps going.

Ben Rowson (11)
Redhills Community Primary School, Exeter

Emotions On The Moon

E motions and feelings swelling up inside
M ums, kids, Dad, wife, will they forget
O nly I, yes, only I made this decision
T ime, time, time, where have you gone
I magination has caught up with me
O h how I miss my mum's Sunday roast
N othing shall stand in my way, I will return
S tars, shooting stars please say that I can return

O n the moon there's nowhere to hide
N othing to hold except rock and dust

T oo many stars in the sky
H ello Mum and Dad, I miss you too much
E veryone look at the meteors, they're like potatoes

M y wife and kids are watching me now
O h I can't even feel my muscles
O h the feeling on the moon is a feeling I've never felt before
N ow I really feel the pain of missing my family.

Chloe Tucker (9)
Redhills Community Primary School, Exeter

Seeing Scenery In The Stars

A s we reach the crumbling moon, as white as a pint of milk, we
S tand here looking at all the other planets,
T hey look amazing, all lonely they stand there spinning around,
R ed as blood, Mars I stand on,
O n an orange planet, the sun an apple, I stand here doing
N othing but I decide to start eating a ham sandwich,
A nd it's like competing in a sport you've never practised, exercise
  and sleeping too!
U nbelievable scenery up here in the shimmering, shiny stars,
T hey look amazing all lonely they,
S tand there, I look at them and see the world, the radio starts to
  break up as we move.

Emma Hunt (10)
Redhills Community Primary School, Exeter

Bad Things In Space

Shocked
Feeling still
Screaming inside
Speech taken
Broken down
In space

Pictures
Meteorite shower
Hit shuttle
Spinning round and round
Heading for no-man's-land
Seeing pictures in my head

Sun
Heading for the sun
NASA can't hear me
Heart pounding
Dead.

Alex Broom (10)
Redhills Community Primary School, Exeter

Space Poem

Broken to death,
Missing family,
Feeling lonely and empty,
And standing very still,
Frozen like an icicle,
Like the ice at the edge of the world.

Darkness, never-ending darkness,
Lost in space,
Jumping up and down,
In space, can't walk,
Heart pounding,
Not what you see in the movies.

Rakan Jumah (10)
Redhills Community Primary School, Exeter

Out Of Space

Speechless,
Unable to jump,
Feel very stiff.

Am I really in space?
Yes,
Watching planets.

Depression,
Thinking of wife,
Cuts like a knife.

Emptiness,
Cold hearted,
Downcast.

Going home,
All alone,
Missing my wife,
As she's my life.

Isabelle Kenyon (10)
Redhills Community Primary School, Exeter

In Space

S hooting stars light up the darkness
P luto waiting for you
A stronauts in the space station flying
C omet surrounded in the air by other planets
E ek, urgent call, don't know what to do

S pace is a wonderful place to go to
T o get there you will need a fast rocket
A stronauts in the air
T o investigate the planet we're not afraid
I n Saturn it is cold and it makes me shiver
O n the Planet Venus the colour is green
N oisy rockets shooting by makes my ears hurt.

Amelia Robbins (10)
Redhills Community Primary School, Exeter

Space

Up in space,
No people to talk,
On the radio,
My only colleagues to talk to,
Alone,
So exhausted,
Heart stops moving.
Broke to death,
Missing family,
Hear voices,
All upset,
Going to die,
Might live,
No oxygen left,
Almost dead,
He will miss the world,
Sadly he died.

Max George (11)
Redhills Community Primary School, Exeter

Asteroid Attack

A steroids charging through the galaxy like an eagle gliding in the sky,
S o big that you could fit the average sized car park into it,
T he moon looking away scared that it could be hit by the huge boulders,
E ntering the Earth's atmosphere,
R acing through the air,
O range, scalding flames blazing from the space rock,
I t's only a matter of time before St Petersburg gets destroyed by the gigantic fireball,
D ashing through the sky like Rudolph and Santa on Christmas Eve, the asteroid makes first contact with the Earth,
S *mash!*

Matthew Coniteer (10)
Redhills Community Primary School, Exeter

Space

All alone,
unable to jump,
I fell over with,
a bump.
As still as a
statue,
no one to talk to,
I was shocked when
I landed on the
moon.
When I stepped into
the shiny rocket it
was gone in a
flash.
And I felt like
I was going to
crash.

Josh Adams (11)
Redhills Community Primary School, Exeter

Space Adventure

A mazing scenery,
S cared I'm going to f-f-freeze up here though,
T alking with my friend about the atmosphere, he said he was a
feather,
R ockets standing still like somebody playing musical statues,
O ver there are the other planets smiling happily,
N ever-ending galaxy that will never stop,
A wful aliens creeping up on me,
U nder my feet is just boring rock that has been there for thousands
of years,
T aking off to Earth, the beautiful Earth, finally going home to my
loved family,
S o, so happy to be home.

Ben Scott (10)
Redhills Community Primary School, Exeter

Space

I looked up at space,
Didn't have some stars too bare.
One thousand I saw.

One thousand stars up.
They're looking at me with shine.
I wished myself there.

Soaring through the clouds.
Meteors coming for me.
Stars burning my eyes.

Planets as big as,
The stars and sun. I was
Filled to the brim with joy.

'Come on down, Judy.
It's time for tea.' I fell with,
No gravity. Dreams.

Tyler-Jae Crawford (10)
Redhills Community Primary School, Exeter

Space Walking

S itting in the large shuttle
P reparing for the moon walk, it's a trampoline
A dding notes I wonder
C an I accomplish my dream to be an astronaut?
E xhilarating, exciting, ending never comes

10, 9, 8, 7, 6, 5, 4, 3, 2, 1 *boom!*

W owed by the power of the bright, golden sun
A llowing myself to float over the Earth
L anding on the moon
K icking space rocks with my weak muscles
I n the light of the sun, I shine as bright as a light
N ever-ending night will not allow light
G etting cold, the moon shivers.

Hannah Dean (10)
Redhills Community Primary School, Exeter

Space Haiku

Into space I zoom,
Faster than an aeroplane,
Past the shining stars.

Through the emptiness,
I am a cheetah running,
Flying through dark space.

Past red-hot comets,
Flying through the vacuum and,
Getting lost in space.

I fly past metal,
It's off the satellites and,
The failed rockets.

One day I'll be back,
To do some experiments,
To get to red Mars.

Emily Padley (11)
Redhills Community Primary School, Exeter

What Am I?

I wear a black coat with silver stripes that sparkle in the sun.
I am big like a New York building.
I'm terrifying like the end of the world.
I am dark as night but also bright like a summer's day.
What am I?
I am silent like an empty classroom.
I sing a song that sounds like thunder.
I eat rocks that are hot like lava.
I have seen World War II and World War I.
This should be a clue, I am out of this world.
I am out of this world because I am in space!
I am watching you right now!

Alesha Rowe (10)
Redhills Community Primary School, Exeter

Guess Who I Am

People say I am never-ending,
I am adventurous,
Out of this world,
I stare at the clouds,
I gaze at the stars,
I can see you dream a dream,
I wear a dull, dim coloured coat with a golden zip,
You can think of me, as a black panther, that spies on planets,
And eats everything in my way,
Do not judge me by that as,
I can be as inviting as a butterfly,
But can be as terrifying as a bull charging at you,
Stars wink at me,
Have you guessed who I am?
Who am I?

I am space!

Taylah Burt (11)
Redhills Community Primary School, Exeter

If I Was . . . I Would

If I was the moon,
I would smile at every child,
If I was a star,
I would twinkle every night,
If I was a planet,
I would dance the night away,
If I was a comet,
I would win the race,
Space is the best,
If I was the sun,
I would be extremely hot,
Space would win my race.

Ellie Tucker (11)
Redhills Community Primary School, Exeter

Planets In Space

P lanets floating up in space like a cloud standing in the sky,
L ying there for you and me so wonderful to see,
A fter we land we shall see stars that are shining bright,
N o one will see much more beauty,
E verything is standing out,
T esting rocks from the glowing, happy moon now *bang, bang, bang*, to get them out,
S pace is beautiful as you can see waiting there for you and me.

I n every exciting planet you see,
N o one else but astronauts will see.

S pecial planets that I can see,
P erfect sight although there's no sound,
A great place for us to see waiting there for you and me,
C razy shaking on the way back to Earth,
E verything that you could dream out in space.

Jessica Beaty (10)
Redhills Community Primary School, Exeter

Beautiful Space

B eaming with excitement whilst I got in the rocket,
E ven though I'm excited I am very scared,
A fter I get into the rocket the countdown starts,
U sing a sick bag to be sick in,
T errible loud noises struck as I landed on the moon,
I n space is great,
F our amazing planets ahead,
U nable to stop floating,
L iving on Earth is not as good as this,

S eeing all of the twinkling stars,
P raying that I will make it back to Earth alive,
A cting like I'm OK, when I am not,
C rowded by breathtaking planets,
E arth is waiting for me to get home.

Rosie-Mae Isaac (10)
Redhills Community Primary School, Exeter

If Space Were An Animal

If space were an animal, what would it be?
If space wore clothes, what would it be?
If space played games, what would it be?
If space sang a song, what would it be?
If space had a house, what would it be?
If space were a man, who would it be?

If space were an animal, it would be a majestic lion standing proud.
If space wore clothes, they would be a huge, black cloak with stars
on its back.
If space played games, they would be tracking asteroids
And swallowing stars and watching them slowly fade
Away into its tummy.
If space sang a song, it would be empty and bare.
If space had a house, it would be big and dark.
If space were a human, he would be senile and judicious.

Jacob Adcock (11)
Redhills Community Primary School, Exeter

Space

Space, stars shining like diamonds in the sky.
Planets spinning all the time, some with rings, some with holes.
Twinkling stars are in the sky happy and fine.
Astronauts flying high in the sky on a big explosive bomb.
Cheerful and delighted to be doing an experiment for Earth
And they think the sun is fun.
Twinkling stars are in the sky happy and fine.
Counting each set of rocks in their heads,
Thinking they're going to be a brilliant astronaut,
Hoping they are not going to be stranded up here where it is never-
ending.
Twinkling stars are in the sky happy and fine.
Excited but worried as well as space is spooky, scary sky
And it is very quiet but the sun is hot and bright,
Twinkling stars are in the sky happy and fine.

Amy Blake (10)
Redhills Community Primary School, Exeter

Space Walking

W ithout gravity it's hard to walk on the dusty moon
A m I going to die?
L ooking around I'm the only one there
K orea and all the other nations look small from here
I 'm on my own out here repairing the space shuttle
N ASA mission control are raiding to see new things
G asping for air in the space station

I t is as black as night all the time
N ew things are yet to be explored

S omersaulting is easy as there is no gravity
P lenty of people have been into space
A ll the time it is like night
C ourageous people go into space
E xercising is essential otherwise you become weak.

Ben Speak (9)
Redhills Community Primary School, Exeter

If Space . . .

If space had eyes, it would see the moon smiling endlessly.
If space wore clothes, it would wear a long, golden, glistening cloak
that twinkled like the stars.
If space had a mouth, it would sing a high-pitched, ear-piercing song
that echoed throughout the endless, dark sky.
If space was an animal, it would be an enormous shark eating
everything within its reach.
If space could look, it would see the scorching sun as hot as a pit of
luminous orange lava beating down on Earth.
If space had ears, it would hear the rocket's engine as noisy as a
school playground that is jam-packed with children.
If space was as hungry as a pack of wolves, it would eat small,
undiscovered planets.

Do you think space could do these things?

Lara Berry (11)
Redhills Community Primary School, Exeter

The Journey Of Space

Space is a dark soul that will take your mind away on a new adventure.
If I travelled in space I would see stars winking and glistening bright.
I would see planets as round as balls with diamond-like eyes.
Comets like shots running and racing towards planets swooping past Earth.
Space wore a dark, black cape that was endless and went on and on and never stopped.
If I travelled in space I would see, the moon staring and smiling at me.
If space were an animal it would be a black panther eating everything in its path swapping its way back to front.

Chloe Melton (10)
Redhills Community Primary School, Exeter

Space

I'm space, who wears a
Black cape with tiny buttons
That sparkle in the sky.

When I'm hungry I
Like eating rockets that come
Flying towards me.

If I could sing I would
Sing a calm song that goes
On and on and on.

Omar Folkes (11)
Redhills Community Primary School, Exeter

Wanting To Know About Space!

S till, silent, soundless space,
P eople have many questions,
A ll about space,
C ould there be aliens on the moon?
E verybody has a question!

What would space wear? A long, black cloak covered in stars?
How would space sing? A song as endless as a bottomless pit?
Anything, what would it eat? A round sphere of cheese?
Tell anyone what you know!

Tyla Jade Bracey (11)
Redhills Community Primary School, Exeter

Space

I'm alone, I'm not at home,
I'm missing my life, is this my life?
I'm not stuck, I'm in luck,
It's awesome here although there's nothing to hear,
I'm cold but I'm bold,
There's so much to see . . .
Between you and me,
The sun is as bright as my mother's smile,
It's like I have the whole world at my fingertips.

Tommy Leahy (11)
Redhills Community Primary School, Exeter

Stars In Space

Stars twinkle like bright green emeralds in the spooky, scary sky.
Painting, glittering, the colour of peach and white.
Sparkling as bright as the yellow sun, bun, drum.
Counting the shiny suns to see how many there are . . . but there are too many of them.
You just can't count them all.
Pretty emeralds are green, it is Christmas tree lights.
The cheerful, dark, black space is the sound of *sshh* . . .

Rheanna Gliddon (10)
Redhills Community Primary School, Exeter

Space Is

Space is as silent as a mouse, but as deafening as two fighting hippos.
Space is as bright as a sunlit, summer's day, but as black as a cold winter's night.
Space is as terrifying as a tiger and panther tearing you to shreds, but as inviting as a lovely chocolate ice cream.
Space is as interesting as learning about King Henry VIII, but as dull as sitting on the sofa for eight hours.

Adam David Jarman (11)
Redhills Community Primary School, Exeter

What's Happening?

Getting in the rocket about to take off,
Shivering and shaking, when the aircraft took off.

Never know what's going to happen, will I die, or will I not?
Eating food is hard to do, it's like a competition between me and you.
All I can hear is the countdown of 5, 4, 3, 2, 1.
Can't stop fidgeting, heart beating faster than a roller coaster.
Never know what's going to happen, will I die, or will I not?

Porscha Louise Bracey (10)
Redhills Community Primary School, Exeter

Space

Space is full of stars.
The sun shines as bright as a firework.
Up there, comets fly as fast as eagles.
Meteors zoom like bullets.
The moon smiles down onto the Earth.
The darkness is like a black panther, striding on and on.
And on and on . . . and never stops.

Emily Collyer (10)
Redhills Community Primary School, Exeter

My Space Experience

Many sparkling stars,
Planets so colourful,
Not for long.
Flying rocks,
Spinning around,
Was I on a roller coaster?
Sick everywhere.

Kelsey Hodge (10)
Redhills Community Primary School, Exeter

Zip Zap Zoom

Zip, zap, zoom, exploring space
Zip, zap, zoom, it's a really cool place
Zip, zap, zoom, stars shine bright
Zip, zap, zoom, only at night
Zip, zap, zoom, rockets roar
Zip, zap, zoom, rockets soar
Zip, zap, zoom, aliens rock
Zip, zap, zoom, aliens bop
Zip, zap, zoom, to the moon
Zip, zap, zoom, be home soon.

Sophie Elmes-Shute
Riverside Community Primary School, Plymouth

Looking For Planets

I look up from Earth and try to see,
The planets looking back at me,
Try and find Mercury, Venus and Mars.

I look anxiously at the Milky Way up in the stars,
Where are Saturn and Neptune?
They're far away like the moon.
Telescope would be the best for spotting Pluto and the rest.

Harley Twigg (9)
Riverside Community Primary School, Plymouth

Out Of This World

Today I saw the solar system playing,
Pluto and Mars were playing hit.
Saturn and Mercury were playing a running game.
Today I saw the planets sobering,
The black hole was left out
Like an abandoned dog.

Jessica Barrett (9)
Riverside Community Primary School, Plymouth

Out Of This World?

Out in space I saw the universe dancing,
stars shining, also twinkling,
twinkling like a
disco ball in
a party or
anniversary for an
eighteen-year-old.

Out in space I saw the universe floating,
the sun as a ref
and the moon
and the Earth running
around the sun,
the moon teasing it
by running around it a ton,
it always took a year for the Earth
and the moon to
go around the race track
of the sun.
They never give up,
it's like an evil person
and a good person fighting
for the land.

Out in space I saw the universe floating,
the sun staying in place
floating like a peregrine falcon
hovering, waiting for its prey
and the Earth spinning
like a merry-go-round
but a lot faster, the moon
just circling around
the Earth like
people huddling
for something good
to happen.

Out in space I saw the universe packed,
people landing on the moon,
also sending robots

to find new planets,
also some orbits
shouting plans
like building
more orbits,
getting ways
to conquer
the universe, to
see what's out there.

Leon Crathorne (9)
Riverside Community Primary School, Plymouth

Amy In Space

In space the
Planets
Rotate rapidly,
Like
Trees in
A breeze.

In space the
Mental Milky Way
Sucks in
Everything,
Like a
Hoover.

In space the
Meteoroids
Race rapidly,
Like a
Racer.

Amy Chambers
Riverside Community Primary School, Plymouth

Out Of This World

When you look up in the sky,
You can't see much with your eye.
Through my telescope look and see,
What's in space high above me.

Giant Jupiter with its moons,
Spinning Saturn with its rings,
Orbiting satellites to keep an eye on things.

When you look up in the sky at night,
You will see the most amazing sight.
Through my telescope look and see,
Stars and planets and galaxies.

Dancing galaxies spiralling with colourful gases,
Black holes feasting on everything in sight.
Luminous, spherical stars like torches shining bright.

When you are up in the sky,
In spaceships you will fly,
Through the window look and see,
How tiny Earth looks beneath me.

Fluffy white clouds that look like sheep,
Mighty mountains surrounded by green trees,
Clear blue serene seas,
Which gently wave in the breeze.

Isabel Rose Lawson (10)
Riverside Community Primary School, Plymouth

Out Of This World

Up, up, up high in the sky I saw the moon rotating
and the sun was lying on its axis
doing nothing, something like an owl in the day
but the sun was as bright as fire
(because it is a big gassy fiery ball).

Last night I heard space rockets zooming
(*zoom, zoom, zoom*) across the galaxy.

Destiny Angel Ann Butterworth (9)
Riverside Community Primary School, Plymouth

Space Rocket

This morning I saw the spaceship zooming through the sky.

The moon crying that poured falling astronauts because it was too loud for them.

Spinning meteors to the Earth as fast as a cheetah can run.

And stars shining sadly.

Ellie Hall-Hutchings
Riverside Community Primary School, Plymouth

Race To The Moon!

In 1966 there was a race to the moon,
Both the Russians and the Americans
Wanted to be there soon.

They started up their engines
And left in a zoom
But for all the Russian knew . . .
They were going to face a terrible
Doom!

The Russian cosmonauts
Travelled home distraught
Because the American astronauts
Had won.

So next time you face a challenge
Believe in yourself
Just like the
Astronauts and cosmonauts.

Seana Hurrell (10)
Riverside Community Primary School, Plymouth

A Poem About Space

Last night I saw the stars twinkling as bright as a big fiery ball of gas
The planets are rotating slowly
The satellite dishes are spinning

Last night I saw the planets spinning round
In circles
Again and again
Getting bored every time
Sun going to bed
Moon is coming out

So look out the window tonight
You just might see a shooting star!

Ellieann Filer (9)
Riverside Community Primary School, Plymouth

What Is Space?

Last night I saw Mars
Sleeping peacefully whilst
The Earth was rotating like a roller coaster.

This morning I saw the sun
Rising, a huge fireball in the sky
As I walk to school I often think how amazing it is
But don't say it as it's not cool!

Tonight the weather will be very clear
I wonder what I will see?
Will everyone be looking, or will it just be me?

So when you go to bed tonight
Be sure to look up high
Cos if you're very lucky
You may see a shooting star
Passing by!

Spencer Coles (9)
Riverside Community Primary School, Plymouth

All About Space!

Sparkling, shooting stars danced
Quickly in the pitch-black darkness of space.

All the comets through the stars were having a race.
When I was little I thought the round, rocky moon was made out of cheese.
But now I know it isn't, if I stand on it I will freeze.

Swirling like a whirlpool, it's called the Milky Way
Just like a ballerina pirouetting every day.

The sun is hot like a ball of fire
It is something you should not admire.

Mars, Mercury, Jupiter, Saturn, all spin around the same way
Together every day.

Tegan Katolina Perry (9)
Riverside Community Primary School, Plymouth

Out Of This World

Last night I saw the dusty and misty, moon playing tag with shiny racing rockets that come carefully to visit him

Last night I saw the twinkling stars colourfully painting the rainbows ready for the bright sun to come outside and the rain to follow

Last night I saw through my terrific telescope, a solid satellite floating around Earth sending signals to each one-and-other person on Planet Earth

Last night I had a dream like I was having sleeping gas and saw the Earth and moon rotating round the galaxy! So colourful and so cool, like I was in a pool . . .

Aidan Pollin (10)
Riverside Community Primary School, Plymouth

What Is Space?

Last night I saw the blaring moon
Looking upon me, as there was a big surprise
An alien was peering at me like a dog wanting to have its bone.

This morning I saw the fearsome sun
Shimmering in my eyes
Some clouds came past – the sun used them as a disguise.

So tonight get ready to make a wish as a bright star might come past
your
Bedroom tonight.

Megan Reid (9)
Riverside Community Primary School, Plymouth

The Solar System

The solar system is no mystery
It's as easy to learn as history
The sun gives the planets light
And the perfect planets keep it until night!

The stars chatter and they shine
Until it is the end of time!
So if you know about Neptune
You'll know as quickly as a cheetah
About the moon!

Courtney Daykin (10)
Riverside Community Primary School, Plymouth

Out Of This World

Last night I saw the meteors winking at the moon,
Jupiter singing a lullaby to the sun,
Mars waking up the stars with spinning satellites all around.
I like to admire them night and day but I wonder why space goes away,
So I go through a tough day until night comes back.
Am I the only one watching the sun,
I hope it's not just me,
Because there's lots more to see than you think.

Ellisha Herd (10)
Riverside Community Primary School, Plymouth

Space

In the magnificent moonlit sky,
Twinkling way up high
Stars danced around
The moon,
And
Put on a show,
They danced and twirled
Like a ballet pirouetting
Twirl, twirl, twirl.

Amelia Ide (9)
Riverside Community Primary School, Plymouth

Aliens

The stars shimmered through
The galaxy like sparkly glitter
Astronauts in the distance . . . they could see the sun
I bet they're having fun.
Aliens putting on a show
I think they need to go
Astronauts think, *should we go? No!*
And they stayed in space forever with the aliens.

Ellie Wadlan (9)
Riverside Community Primary School, Plymouth

Space Chimps, Dogs And Others

Ham was the first chimp in space,
He had the right sort of face,
Ham had his own suit,
It was so cute!
His rocket had a port hole,
It looked quite good as he set off from the universe's soul,
His lift-off started with a rumble,
He was a little way from the jungle.

Laika was the first dog in space,
She travelled to an unknown place,
Her attendance meant she went into orbit,
She arrived on the moon alright,
But she got quite a fright.

Luca was the first cat in space,
He had lots of mice to chase,
His people were so very proud,
They really were a crowd,
He landed on the moon so soon,
The rocket launched as swift as a balloon.

So all of these animals have been to space,
And all of them so brave,
All of them have achieved targets,
So next time you think of space,
Think of all of the targets
It took to gape into the solar system.

Kitty Parekh (10)
St Ives Junior School, St Ives

What's Up There?

I look up at the dark, night sky,
What can I see?
The stars, the planets,
And the man on the moon smiling back at me.

I know that there are galaxies,
Ours is the Milky Way,
Bands of stars that sweep the sky,
You can't see it during the day.

Mercury is the closest planet to our big sun,
It is really hot,
But not the hottest one.

Venus is the hottest,
Because of how it's made,
Even though it's not the closest,
Don't expect any shade.

Earth is the planet that we know so much about,
We are very lucky,
That there is no doubt.

Mars is the red one and has a moon or two,
People think there could be life,
If only we knew.

Jupiter is the biggest,
And largest of them all,
One of the gas giants,
None of them are small.

Saturn is the only one,
That has some visible rings,
These are made of rock and ice,
And lots of other things.

Uranus is a funny one,
Because it's on its side,
A meteor the size of Earth,
Knocked it on its ride.

Neptune is so cold, dark,
And full of mystery,

But there used to be another one,
According to history.

But it can no longer be called a planet,
Due to its small size,
Pluto is now a dwarf planet,
And is happy in the skies.

So now we've found out a bit about space,
We know what it is like,
I just can't wait to find out more,
And maybe visit and take a hike.

Harvey O'Dell (9)
St Ives Junior School, St Ives

Happy Galaxy

Here I lie,
Up in the sky,
Shining so bright,
Looking down in delight.

Golden and bronze I burn away,
Until my daylight fades away.

Now here is my mate,
Not too late,
White and round,
On Earth he does bound,
Silver and shiny,
Cor, he's far from tiny,
Way up high,
'Til morning is nigh.

Our friends with twinkles and smiles,
Who will know between the miles,
They sparkle and glisten,
I'm sure they do listen,
For as I lay,
To await the next day.

Lewis Rebeiro (10)
St Ives Junior School, St Ives

Zooming Through Space

When I was zooming through space
I saw Jupiter and he said,
'Hey, I'm Jupiter, I like to hip hop
And I sing every day at exactly 4 o'clock.'

When I was shooting through space
I saw Uranus and he said,
'Hi, I'm Uranus, I say that with pride,
No wait, I lied, I'm the only planet spinnin' on my side.'

When I was flying through space
I saw Earth and she sang,
'Aloha, I'm Earth,
My power comes from the sun
And everyone around me likes having fun.'

When I was sailing through space
I saw Venus and she said,
'Hello, I'm Venus, the planet of love
And I like to spin backwards in the heavens above.'

When I was rocketing through space
I saw Mars and he said,
'Oi, I'm Mars, I'm made up of rust
And when your planet goes bang
I'm the one you can trust.'

Jozie Uys (10)
St Ives Junior School, St Ives

What Am I?

I only come out at night
I am an atom
I am bigger than other planets.

I am very twinkly and glittery
And I shine very brightly
I am a star.

Millie Upton (10)
St Ives Junior School, St Ives

The Aliens Are Coming!

What are these things flying overhead?
While the children stay put, snug in their beds,
Their faces like fire,
Their shuttles pure sapphire.

Their ships land, quiet as night,
Are we all ready to put up a fight?
'Retreat!' comes the shout,
And we all run about,
Twisting, twirling,
Spiralling, swirling.

I look up at the great, golden orb in the sky,
'Wait!' I hear myself cry,
These things could be good for all we know,
We don't know how far our relations could go.

I walk forward cautiously to shake their hands,
So does the head of the new species band,
Suddenly from their pockets they draw . . . guns!
Quickly as lightning we turn and run.

Grab the children from their beds,
Heaven knows what's in their heads?
It seems the aliens will be our foe,
So let's get out – go, go, go!

Charlie Harvey (10)
St Ives Junior School, St Ives

An Alien's View

Here they go again, the 'human' race,
Zooming around at a snail's pace.
Searching, seeking, trying to find me,
Sometimes I have to hide behind Mercury.
Maybe one day, I'll have to show my face,
But until then I'll hide in space!

Indie Theodore (9)
St Ives Junior School, St Ives

The Super Solar System

Space, space is full of grace,
It's so lovely to see this,
This amazing place.

Up here, I soar on my rocket flight,
I can view the whole world,
Such an incredible sight.

All the planets in the galaxy,
Shine so bright,
For all to see.

Full moon, half moon or crescent,
Each time I see it,
It's the best Christmas present.

The stars,
They are glowing,
Just truly mind-blowing.

The golden burning sun,
Always has its perfect shine,
Oh how I wish it was mine, all mine.

Layla Bolton (9)
St Ives Junior School, St Ives

Shine Bright

I've always wondered about the stars,
How they always shine so bright,
And when I look outside my window,
I see such a wonderful sight.

The beautiful stars,
They shine so bright,
They're always wonderful to see.

But when I want to reach up high,
I'll never get to where they lie.

Amber Rose Hudson (10)
St Ives Junior School, St Ives

Space Rats

You better not mess with the rats
They're really, really long like mats
Their teeth are like daggers
You need to keep away from them.

You better keep away from the rats
They can sting for days
Rats can really bite but these really hurt.

They jump up to your head
They bite your legs
They chew you to bits
They rip you to pieces.

They're not nice rats
They look like cats
And they're really, really fat.

So now you know what they are
Just be careful
You could find them on Earth.

Marcus Hughes (9)
St Ives Junior School, St Ives

Exploring Space

S piralling in space all by myself,
O nly little food makes me not have good health,
L ives at homes are different from my living life here,
A round the corner a few miles away a planet is coming near,
R ealising I had to get away I turn my thrusters on,

S tars rush past me, phew the planet is nearly gone,
Y ou never quite know what is out here with me,
S atellites, asteroids or even ET,
T ravelling in space I feel all alone,
E arth here I come, it's time to phone home,
M um, get the kettle on, I'm here, I'm home and I'm no longer alone.

Sienna Hamm (10)
St Ives Junior School, St Ives

Cosmic Trip

All aboard the bus on our cosmic trip of a lifetime,
Take a seat and enjoy our planet rhyme.
Let's go!
First past Neptune and Uranus
Now onto super Saturn and its rough rings,
Carrying on to ginormous Jupiter.
Wow, we've travelled far,
That's a lot of things.
Next to marvellous Mars, past the comets
And past the stars,
A hop, skip and a jump
And Earth is in sight,
Then to Venus always a delight.

Next to last on our trip is magnificent Mercury
I like a bit of light,
We've reached the end of our trip
As we land on the hot, red sun,
Now it's time to end our fun.

Arwen Merrill (10)
St Ives Junior School, St Ives

A Little White Star

A little white star shines a bright light.
Oh it was a beautiful sight.
It sparkled and twinkled,
My fingertips tingled,
Maybe I'll go to space.

I'll rush and I'll race,
I'll pack my suitcase.
I'm all packed
And ready to go.
Oh no, no, no, I just can't go,
I don't have a rocket to fly in!

Isabelle Fellows-Barnett (10)
St Ives Junior School, St Ives

Star Constellations

S piralling galaxies dance in the night sky
T rillions of worlds within, appearing to fly
A rchers of the sky shooting far and wide
R eigning down upon us, Sagittarius fires with pride

C anis Major, a greater dog
O ver above Earth's thick, thick fog
N eon beacons blazing, Sirius and Vega
S hiny, brightest of them all, even Ursa Major
T errifyingly raging in the heavens above us
E ntering the sky, his name Taurus,
L ion slumbering through the dark
L eo prowling and hunting like a shark
A ndromeda originating from Greek mythology
T he chained lady listed by astronomer, Ptolemy
I magination of making these constellations
O riginal by the Greeks and Sumerians
N octurnal, being up in space
S uns or stars make up each face.

Farrah Searle (10)
St Ives Junior School, St Ives

Space Through My Eyes

Planets swirling in outer space,
Comets zooming across the night sky,
Oh the universe, what a wonderful place!
We look up, up, up high.

We see the moon, the stars and the Milky Way,
The sun, the fizzing, whizzing, bubbling ball of gas,
All of this millions of light years away,
From Earth with its seas, lakes and land mass.

When I raise my eyes to space,
My heart beats and a smile spreads across my face.

Finn Scott-Anderson (9)
St Ives Junior School, St Ives

Space Adventure

I dreamed I flew a space rocket
Way up in the sky,
White, fluffy clouds went drifting as I flew by.
I saw the sun, I saw the stars, I saw the Milky Way,
To get there it would take forever and a day.

Fiery Mars is a sight to behold,
But space can be so frightfully cold.
Mighty Saturn's rings seem to sparkle and glow,
Our Planet Earth looks so tiny down below.

A meteor, a shooting star zooms into sight,
Shining like a diamond ring, super bright.
Stars and planets spinning into space,
All displayed in front of my face.

I land in my back field,
Those memories I will keep sealed.
I jump back into my warm bed,
My mum came in. 'Night-night,' she said.

Amelia Nelson (10)
St Ives Junior School, St Ives

Cosmic Planets

Among his siblings Mercury is speedy fast,
Compared to Neptune who always is last,
Venus is extremely hot.

While life-supporting Earth
Has a comfortable spot,
Mars' surface is very rocky,
About his size Jupiter is cocky.

Saturn always surrounded by his ring,
While Uranus is strange because of many things.

Alice Zhang (10)
St Ives Junior School, St Ives

Dumb Ways To Die In Space

Take your helmet off in space,
Then everything explodes in your face.
Lose control of a rocket,
And then don't move out the way of a comet.

Dumb ways to die,
So many dumb ways to die.
Dumb ways to die,
So many dumb ways to die.

Poke an alien in the eye,
So then you watch him eat you alive,
Lose contact with mission control,
Then tumble into a huge black hole.

Dumb ways to die,
Dumbest ways to die,
Dumb ways to die,
So many dumb ways to die.

Alice Jones (9)
St Ives Junior School, St Ives

The Solar System

The shape of the solar system is like a plate,
With the planets all different sizes and colours,
Mercury is the planet closest to the sun,
Venus is not nice with gases and acid,
Mars is red and very cold as it is so far from the sun,
Jupiter is the biggest planet of all,
Saturn is the easiest to recognise,
Uranus is the only planet on its side
And is four times bigger than Earth,
Neptune has at least eight moons
And is the coldest planet in our solar system,
Earth does not stay still in space
It travels round and round the sun.

Amy Brewer (9)
St Ives Junior School, St Ives

Chocolate Sweets

Chocolate melting in the galaxy as the magic stars twinkle high in the sky
The stars twinkle like a shining light in the sky
Orbiting the sun every year the Earth travels round
Clouds slowly moving across the night sky on top of the stars
Over the whole world stars light up the sky
Looking up at the night sky to see the wonderful stars
At night the stars twinkle like the sun shining
Twinkling throughout the sky
Ending as the sun rises.

Sleepy children lie in their beds
Or watching the Milky Way swirl
Every person can catch a glimpse
Evening stars or flying saucers
Then tired heads rest on pillows
Sleeping and dreaming of chocolate and sweets.

Olivia Robertson (9)
St Ives Junior School, St Ives

Untitled

Dark, cold emptiness,
Space,
Vast, twinkling scariness,
Space,
Mysterious, spellbinding tranquillity,
Space,
Exquisite, dazzling reflectiveness,
Space,
Blazing, radiant enchantment,
Space,
Bleak, boundless nothingness,
Space,
Eerie, mesmerising incandescence,
Space!

Ben Roderts (10)
St Ives Junior School, St Ives

Stars Twinkling In The Night Sky, See What Comes Flying By

Boom! Bang!
There went the rocket,
Shooting through the luminous sky,
Whizz! Pop!
There it goes, storming to outer space,
I hope they do not die,
I'm sure they won't.

Let's watch them fly away,
Up so high till we can see them no more,
I wonder what they will do on their spaceship stay,
Maybe they will meet an alien or three or four.

Will it be blue? Will it be green?
I don't know, how about you?
Perhaps it will nick a ride back down to Earth!

Andrew Simpson (10)
St Ives Junior School, St Ives

Zurg To Earth

There was an alien called Zurg, who wanted to visit Earth,
He had a green body, he had a long nose,
And he had a pimple on his toe,
He flew down in a rocket, with two pens in his pocket,
When he got to Earth the special thread in his pocket made a big wallet,
He looked in his pocket,
Magically there were two pounds in his pocket
And he put them in his wallet,
Spent the pounds on a proper rocket,
That proper rocket flew him around,
Right down Forth Street and into town,
Over the harbour and into the sky,
Zurg looked back and sighed.

India Alanis Lewis (9)
St Ives Junior School, St Ives

I Am Space

I am space time and sound,
The almighty presence that knows no bounds,
Peppered in stars like diamonds in the night,
Shimmering, twinkling, burning bright.

My gentle hum makes a soothing sound,
Drowned in space junk, whizzing around,
Shooting stars, hot and fast,
Soon burn out, they never last.

Big black hole a hidden trap,
Once inside there's no way back,
Mysterious planets, no signs of life,
War of the worlds would just bring strife.

Planet Earth, a sapphire bold,
So many promises to unfold.

Ruby McMahon (10)
St Ives Junior School, St Ives

Alien Apocalypse!

Yo!
When there's an alien invasion don't panic
Just call alien busters
Yeah!
Now there's a chance of survival
Let's go
When there's a chance alien invasion
You don't tremble
You just call alien killers
Don't scream, don't run
Call alien busters
Yeah!
Now there is a creature
Lurking everywhere
Now there is an alien apocalypse!

Spencer Comley (10)
St Ives Junior School, St Ives

Space Pup

My pup is magic
My pup is great
He does things you won't believe
Like ride a bike and roller skate!

We are going to space
We made a rocket
1, 2, 3, we can't stop it!
Zoom, whizz, bang!
Our adventure has begun!

Through the constellation we fly
Seeing extraterrestrial life,
We bounce on Saturn's rings
Eat a pancake from the saucepan
And cuddle the teddy bear.

Jack Trevorrow (10)
St Ives Junior School, St Ives

Black Hole

Beautiful yet deadly,
Like a snow leopard protecting her cubs,
You cannot escape its wrath,
Looking for you waiting, expecting!

Swirling, twirling, whirling,
Expanding, engulfing,
Dragging anything in its path,
Its hunger ever growing, feeding its empty grasp.

You get swept,
Into a vast vortex of gloom and death,
Always evolving, forever enhancing,
On an unrelenting, never-ending quest.

The all-consuming, ever-entrancing black hole.

Rachael Ruth Beckerleg (10)
St Ives Junior School, St Ives

Lost In Space

We're unfound like galaxies,
We're past the solar system wall,
And head to head with fatalities,
We are not visible at all.

Cartwheeling like gymnastics,
The black hole approaches quick,
Us and the shuttle are still enthusiastic,
To get beyond Pluto before you can click.

Spiralling into the nothingness,
We began to realise,
We are lost in space,
The whole universe in front of our eyes.

Tara Faye Langley (10)
St Ives Junior School, St Ives

Observing

Staring up from Earth I try to see,
The planets glimpsing back at me.
Gazing at gleaming and glistening stars,
I explore for Mercury, Venus and Mars.

Peering at the Milky Way opening up high,
I focus on constellations in the dark sky.
Where are Uranus, Saturn and Neptune?
They're far away, somewhere well beyond the moon.

A telescope would be the best,
For spotting Jupiter and the rest.
But the pinprick patterns and lasting twinkles,
Will keep me mesmerised beyond my wrinkles.

Eloise Horsell (10)
St Ives Junior School, St Ives

Mysterious Space

Stars shooting, sun shining, comets flying,
Rockets soaring, nine orbiting planets one by one,
Constantly moving around a hot fiery sun,
Stars dying but still shining bright enough for us
To see here on Earth happily.

Satellites falling, gravity pulling, Venus bubbling,
Neptune storming, magical mysteries still to be found
By NASA here on the ground.

Scientists, students, astronauts,
There is still so much for us to learn,
Keep on burning Sun,
Burn! Burn! Burn!

Piran Monaghan (10)
St Ives Junior School, St Ives

The Stars

The twinkling, blinking brightness of them,
The magical, breathtaking beauty of them,
The vibrant, marvellous glow of them,
The stars!

The glamorous, glimmering beam of them,
The outstanding, dazzling magic of them,
The colossal, mammoth size of them,
The stars!

The mind-boggling jaw-dropping age of them,
The burning, shrivelling heat of them,
The fiery, warming colour of them,
The incredible, fantastic stars!

Merryn Sophia Vennelle Hichens (9)
St Ives Junior School, St Ives

Mission To Mars

Boom! A rocket went off today
To explore the Milky Way
All the astronauts have been working hard
And they're going very far.

They are going to land on Mars
To cover some of its parts
We see the speck of a star
Shining when they land on Mars.

When we're going home from Mars
We will travel very fast
Like the speed of light or a flaming asteroid
When we get home from Mars.

Fabien Hamon-Lawrence (9)
St Ives Junior School, St Ives

Stars

A peaceful blanket of fluorescent stars,
Looking like a million eyes,
Blinking out of nowhere.
Shooting stars,
Zooming across the midnight sky,
Looking like surfers riding a wave.

A golden beam of light,
Shining a million miles away,
Looking like an . . . explosion!

Mia Claire Lackey (9)
St Ives Junior School, St Ives

Jupiter

Jupiter's circle is a storm,
For 350 years it has swarm,
Jupiter is the biggest planet of them all,
It's even bigger than your school hall.

Jupiter is the fifth planet from the sun,
Don't land on it or you'll be done!
Be careful you'll fall right through,
And then you will die of the flu!

Harley Oliver Mansell (9)
St Ives Junior School, St Ives

Solar System!

Spinning, swirling, shooting about,
All the planets with no doubt.
Beware, beware black holes,
Stare before you blink, your life will be space.
Zooming, looming, zipping through space,
Orange, red, yellow flames bursting out.
Eclipse, eclipse, every few years,
Tears of joy when it is near.

Abbie Alford (9)
St Ives Junior School, St Ives

Space

S uper stars sparkling up high in the velvet night sky
P iercing light from the moon, shining on the vast sea
A wesome astronauts actually landing on the moon
C osmic constellations stretched across the universe
E pic extraterrestrial life extending around space (that's if you are a
   believer).

Lilly Webber (9)
St Ives Junior School, St Ives

Black Hole!

Life-sucker
Light-swallower
Star-killer
Space-eater
Planet-spinner
Dark-murderer
Rocket-ripper
Asteroid-splitter.

Jee Curnew (9)
St Ives Junior School, St Ives

Vostok 1

Yuri Gagarin, first man in space
Thinking what a wondrous place
Gazing down at the glistening Earth
Appearing to be sapphire first.
Lying beside the desolate moon
Easily mistaken for a Spanish doubloon.
Comets are racing through space and time
Heading towards Earth, will we survive.

Grace Baker (9)
St Ives Junior School, St Ives

Spacetastic

S lit leaping across the magical, magnificent moon
P irouetting around the stupendous solar system
A erialing around the scorching sun
C artwheeling on Saturn's rocky ring
E lite is the Earth, it's the best place to be.

Abigail Williams (9)
St Ives Junior School, St Ives

Space Is A Place

Space is a place,
No one wants to go.
Out of the galaxy you will be,
In a black hole.
You will go,
Don't go on.

Kyle Kelly (9)
St Ives Junior School, St Ives

Solar System

Home to all the main planets,
Astronauts up there to explore for extraterrestrial life,
No gravity in space,
We float and jump very high,
Taking years to get to the closest planet.

Ruby Rebecca Leigh Hall (9)
St Ives Junior School, St Ives

The Solar System

Silly Saturn spins the solar system.
Mercury and Mars move magically around the sun.
Excellent Earth is an extraordinary place to live.
Jolly Jupiter jumps like a juggling ball.
Volcanic Venus vibrates vertically.

Joshua Dain (9)
St Ives Junior School, St Ives

The Septic Space Poem

Blazing boulders whizzing through the vast emptiness,
Mysterious mysteries lurking behind
Every single star or maybe behind our planet.
Menacing meteors zipping across the darkness,
Ripping everything in its path.

Harrison Goodman (10)
St Ives Junior School, St Ives

Astro Dog

There was a case when a dog went to outer space.
He went to get away from the human race.
The little scamp went spinning around the solar system.
He first went to Mercury and then on to Mars.
When he was done exploring he went home to Earth to eat.

Isabelle Dain (9)
St Ives Junior School, St Ives

Seasons

Fiery red hedges
A blanket of auburn leaves
Trees smothered with pears.

Snowflakes drifting down
A cloth of sparkling ice
A deer trotting by.

Dainty snowdrops sway
Bluebells nodding to the sun
A carpet of blue.

Summer golden sun
Glossy green grass glistening
Puffy cotton clouds.

Charlotte Miller (10)
St Margaret's Preparatory School, Calne

Back In Time

Through the years back in time
I saw a dog high with slime
Then I saw a sign that said:
Naughty boars with creepy claws,
Running round the pointless doors

Through the years back in line
I saw an Anglo-Saxon thin as a pine
Then I had a closer look
That took me back into the woods

Through the years back in time
I saw a Celt eating limes
Then I saw a sign that said:
Crazy cats smelling like rotten rats,
Chasing silly jumping bats

Through the years back in line
I saw a witch crossing the shire
Then I had a closer look
That took me back to Wiltshire.

Aurora Vergani (9)
St Margaret's Preparatory School, Calne

Autumn

The trees are becoming bare,
As the sunset coloured leaves drift onto the ground,
The air's becoming icy,
And the lakes have frozen over,
A big layer of thick frost covers the ground,
Making everything turn snowy white.
The smoke coming from every chimney around,
The cold dark empty streets forming as night falls,
The bitter air closing in around us,
Mother says, 'Winter's coming,
It'll get colder soon.'

Hannah Browning (9)
St Margaret's Preparatory School, Calne

The Planets Above

Bang, bang! Fire it up
Shooting through the sky
To infinity and beyond
Comets flying
Stars alight
The world around us
Getting smaller by night.

Bang, bang! Fire it up
Mercury not far below
The sun closing in on us
Blinding us by the minute
One small step for Man
One giant leap for mankind
He said, so if he can, we can.

Bang, bang! Fire it up
Beep, beep, petrol light
Oh no! Our last night
Flying back down to Earth
Through the shooting sky
Lights flicker then turn off
Maybe it was fun but still a terrible fly.

Catherine Vaughan (10)
St Margaret's Preparatory School, Calne

The Old House

Down the road is a creepy old house
Down the road lives a mean biting mouse
In the house is an old creaking door
In the shadows a monster will roar
If you open that creepy old door
You will see a big scary claw
Next you will see a hairy foot
Covered with ebony black soot
Then you will see the monster's wife
So make sure you run for your life!

Abigail Wood (7)
St Margaret's Preparatory School, Calne

Who Am I?

I walk like a monkey,
I talk like a bear,
I act like a child,
But I really don't care,
I fit garage doors,
I like to hug, squeeze and scare,
I hide my dancing very well,
But I do lots of dares,
Can you figure it out yet?
OK, it's Brian Holyoake, my dad.

Harriet Holyoake (9)
St Margaret's Preparatory School, Calne

Deep, Deep, Down

Deep, deep, down, down, down
Monsters howl,
As they howl, they howl,
So naughty and foul.
Deep, deep, deep, down, down, down
Where spiders creep,
Creep, creep, creep,
Hanging on cobwebs so dusty and filthy
Ohhhhh!
Ghosts, ghosts,
Haunting
Spooky!
Deep, deep down.

Ariella White (9)
St Margaret's Preparatory School, Calne

A Mystifying Journey

A mystifying journey, in a submarine,
Floating underwater like a mystery dream.
A mystifying journey, to a hidden land,
Shimmering scales, golden sand.
A mystifying journey, help! There's a shark!
False alarm, it's just a shadow in the dark.
A mystifying journey, bubbles floating by,
We're so deep you cannot see the sky.
A mystifying journey, we're starting to rise,
I'm sorry the journey's over, I can see the pale blue skies.

Naia Searight (9)
St Margaret's Preparatory School, Calne

Gruesome Aliens

G reat big comets soar through the sky
R acing meteor showers or
U nidentified flying objects
E xit our solar system
S urprisingly big planets
O bviously tower over the rest
M ysterious things happen up there
E dible cheese, is it the moon?

A mazing sights to see
L oving aliens or so they seem
I nterested in the moon they see
E xploring the Earth
N earby this place you see
S ilently coming and going we will never see.

Callum Pike (10)
St Michael's CE Primary School, Newton Abbot

Sparkling Stars

S aucers spinning
P lanets turning
A stronauts bouncing
R ockets zooming
K nowledge of outer space
L ight years passing
I ncredible sights
N orth, up, up and away
G iant steps, *stomp, stomp!*

S tars twinkling
T rips to outer space
A liens adventuring
R acing across the Milky Way
S pace never-ending.

Alex Davey (10)
St Michael's CE Primary School, Newton Abbot

Shoot Up

Shoot up, shoot up,
The stars go.
Shoot up, shoot up,
That's the way they grow.

Stars are beautiful and shiny too,
People make wishes with you.
Star light, star bright,
First star I see tonight,
I wish I may, I wish I might
Have this wish I wish tonight.
Amazing planets and stars
Tonight they represent space
And fight, fight, fight.

Morgan Bradford (10)
St Michael's CE Primary School, Newton Abbot

Our Solar System

E arth is a place full of creatures and people
A wesome animals roam the land
R abbits hop up and down
T ime goes by and passes away
H appy people laugh, learn and play

S uper speedy rocks fly through the sky
P owerful planets circle the sun
A mazing aliens live in space
C omets shoot around the system
E pic Earth flies through the sky.

Tyler Barnett (10)
St Michael's CE Primary School, Newton Abbot

Space

Space, as hard as rock
Make a wish tonight
Shooting stars shoot up
Bright into the night sky
The stars sparkle bright tonight
The aliens watch them shine tonight
Rockets *whoosh, whoosh!*
Get up, get up, watch the moon shine
Come celebrate tonight
You are all good tonight, sleep tight.

Courtney Bush (10)
St Michael's CE Primary School, Newton Abbot

The Universe

U nder the moon shadow
N ight turns into day
I watch the gleaming stars
V enus glows bright
E arth is shining blue and green
R ushing stars shoot across the sky
S hooting space rockets go high into outer space
E arth's glowing blue sea.

Alfie Abbott (10)
St Michael's CE Primary School, Newton Abbot

The Space Invaders

U nidentified flying objects
N ot possible to see
I nformation tells us that these
V erified objects can fly
E arth is safe but
R un away if they come
S ooner or later they will come, it will be the
E nd of Earth.

Harry Horder (10)
St Michael's CE Primary School, Newton Abbot

The Universe

U nder the dark moon
N umber of stars
I nside a space rocket
V enus vs Pluto
E arth is amazing
R ough dark moon
S hooting stars
E normous universe.

Harry Brewin (11)
St Michael's CE Primary School, Newton Abbot

Space

S tars shine in space like silver
P ersevering planets float endlessly in space
A lphabetical space computers watch over Mars like a bear
watching its cubs
C *rack*, rockets quickly break apart
E xposed Earth is a habitat to humans like a burrow which is a
habitat to rabbits.

Katie Bovey (10)
St Michael's CE Primary School, Newton Abbot

Space

S hooting stars go across at night
P lanets are as small as a piece of chocolate
A s black as a cat
C omets cross the sky at night
E xciting explorers.

Catherine Gilbert (11)
St Michael's CE Primary School, Newton Abbot

Stars

S pace is brilliant like a star
T he stars are as bright as diamonds
A t night as black as a cat
R unning around on the moon having fun
S oon the sun will come again.

Stella Jane Knapp (11)
St Michael's CE Primary School, Newton Abbot

Space

S uper sun
P ure Pluto
A mazing asteroid
C ore of the comet
E ntering Earth once again.

Chay Meathrel (11)
St Michael's CE Primary School, Newton Abbot

Space Poem

S hooting stars flying through the dark sky
P lanes are gliding through the pitch-black sky
A mazing astronauts in rapid rockets
C omets in space
E arth is a lovely planet.

Ewan Bray (10)
St Michael's CE Primary School, Newton Abbot

Space

S o high up in the sky
P luto, Mars, Venus
A nd the white Milky Way
C entre of the Earth
E ntering space again, so scary but exciting in a way.

Louis Fewings (10)
St Michael's CE Primary School, Newton Abbot

Space

S ee all the bright stars.
P lanets to explore.
A mong the stars planets to see.
C ycling around the sun.
E xciting and unexciting stars still bright and far.

Adam Rivers (10)
St Michael's CE Primary School, Newton Abbot

Space

S pace is a fact-finding place
P lanets spin around in space
A s the stars shoot about Earth moves around
C ircling Earth in space
E xciting comets in space.

Corey Edward Parry (10)
St Michael's CE Primary School, Newton Abbot

Space

S hiny stars sparkle like gold
P luto is a dwarf planet
A liens dance on space endlessly
C ollapsing rockets shattering into space
E ight different-sized planets in space.

Kelly Marshall (10)
St Michael's CE Primary School, Newton Abbot

Earth

E arth is magic, it is endless fun
A wesome adventures, every new sun
R oller coasters for our sense of fright
T he Earth is guarded with all its might
H appy people hiding all around, we love our life.

Connor Cox (11)
St Michael's CE Primary School, Newton Abbot

Out Of Space

Stars shine bright in the jet-black sky
While spaceships fly by
The people saying hi as they're loving their time
As they go and find space's wonderful places.

Jack Upsher (11)
St Michael's CE Primary School, Newton Abbot

A Journey In Space

A mazing avalanches of rocks,

J ewels in the sky,
O range glowing sun in the distance,
U ranus is beautiful; we must be quite high,
R ocks are cracking on the moon's surface,
N orthern Lights glow rainbow tonight,
E lectric, flashing sparks of lightning,
Y ou might even see the Milky Way!

I nteresting, incredible, enormous abyss,
N eil Armstrong was first to walk on the moon,

S wirling, spiralling galaxies, what a pretty sight!
P etrifying planets spin in the darkness,
A steroids are starting to fall with a big bang!
C omets and shooting stars are falling swiftly,
E veryone is extremely excited to explore this wonderful place!

Ellie Fennell
St Wilfrid's School, Exeter

Black Holes

B lue and white is our wonderful world
L ight there is little and life there is none
A mazing peace lies upon me as I see a glittering galaxy
C omets crashing down onto beautiful Mother Nature
K nowing that they are indestructible I stare and gaze

H umongous asteroids and debris, pieces crash and tumble
O nly gravity controls us in this extraordinary world
L ook outside and see a glimmering galaxy
E cstatic excitement and I want to go outside
S hooting stars streak across the vast expanse of outer space!

David Antwi
St Wilfrid's School, Exeter

Medusa

Hideous, horrible hag
Tusks as sharp as knives
Frightening snakes and bloodshot eyes
Leathery wings as long as a person
Medusa, Medusa, Medusa.

Disgusting, ugly crone
Snakes dancing like flames
Terrifying, scaly skin
Hands like claws
Medusa, Medusa, Medusa.

Nasty, vile creature
Black protruding tongue
Sharp knife-like claws
Tusks like a boar
Medusa, Medusa, Medusa.

Elisha Andrew (9)
Shakespeare Primary School, Plymouth

The Beautiful Princess

There was once a beautiful princess
With eyes as blue as the sea,
And hair as long as Rapunzel's that shone so beautifully.
She lived in a castle so far and wide,
She was going to be an amazing bride.
Unfortunately things weren't as they seemed.
The princess' stepmother was very very mean
The princess was locked in the tallest tower
Because the stepmother had a magical power.
One fine day a prince came running
With swords in the air and was very cunning.
He came to the rescue of the princess,
To take her away from all the evilness.
The prince snuck in and saved the princess.
They left the castle in an awful mess.

Katie Rendle (8)
Shakespeare Primary School, Plymouth

Medusa

Pointed, revolting, repulsive teeth
Pitch-black but somehow piercing white eyes
Demonic, tedious thoughts
Scales as hard as an alligator
But as smooth as a viper's
Black, dark, cold heart
Medusa, Medusa, Medusa.

Crimson venomous blood drooping down
Out of hungry snakes' terrible jaws
Stunning vile face
Death, gore written everywhere
Leathery, hideous wings
Filthy hag
Medusa, Medusa, Medusa.

Regan Boateng (9)
Shakespeare Primary School, Plymouth

My Cats

I have two cats,
One of my cats is called Billy
And he sometimes acts silly.
My other cat is called Tinkerbell
And we get on very well.
Both of my cats are black,
With very big green eyes,
Tinkerbell likes to purr a lot,
But Billy always cries.
My cats have black tails
And big fluffy black paws,
And little white sharp teeth, inside their jaws.
They make loud noises when they purr,
Especially when I rub their fur!

Emily Blackburn (7)
Shakespeare Primary School, Plymouth

Medusa

Dreadful, vile creature,
Slimy, hissing snakes,
Deadly, black, creepy eyes,
Teeth as sharp as daggers.

Scales dark green colour,
Slimy all over,
Like a serpent,
Medusa, Medusa, Medusa.

Eyes as creepy as a black hole,
Green, hideous scales,
Tongue so pointy,
Medusa, Medusa, Medusa.

Madison Collihole (9)
Shakespeare Primary School, Plymouth

Medusa

Vicious old crone
Scales like a dragon
Knife-like claws as sharp as a shark's teeth
Medusa, Medusa, Medusa.

Tusks like a boar's
Horrible old hag
Giant legs, hairy armpits
Medusa, Medusa, Medusa.

Smelly hostile thing
Pythons for hair
One look would turn you to stone
Medusa, Medusa, Medusa.

Jack Wilton (9)
Shakespeare Primary School, Plymouth

Medusa

Dreadful, loathsome creature
Scaly body like a boa constrictor
Claws as sharp as daggers
Snakes that wriggle on her head
Medusa, Medusa, Medusa

Tusks as big as a boar
Ugly old crone
Vile skin
Nasty creature
Hideous features
Turn you to stone
Medusa, Medusa, Medusa.

Leah Quayle (10)
Shakespeare Primary School, Plymouth

Medusa

Hideous, vile, bloodthirsty hag,
Tusks like a boar's,
Snakes wiggling like flames,
Black tongue,
Grotesque skin
Medusa, Medusa, Medusa.

Claws like daggers,
Dangerous teeth,
Vile breaths,
Snotty nose,
Gross skin
Medusa, Medusa, Medusa.

Stephin Jones (10)
Shakespeare Primary School, Plymouth

Medusa

Snakes dancing like flames,
Fingernails like claws,
Ebony feathery wings,
Horrible, vicious hag,
Medusa, Medusa, Medusa.

Scaly, slimy skin,
Ebony black tongue,
Staring eyes like crystal balls,
Dark black, rotten dagger teeth,
Medusa, Medusa, Medusa.

Kirsty Ward (9)
Shakespeare Primary School, Plymouth

Medusa

Dreadful, disgusting hag
Scaly body like a viper
Big leathery wings
Enormous tusks like a boar's
Medusa, Medusa, Medusa.

Ugly, unattractive features
Sharp knife-like claws
Grotesque old crone
Writhing mass of snakes on her head
Medusa, Medusa, Medusa.

Summer McNair (9)
Shakespeare Primary School, Plymouth

Medusa

Hideous, savage hag
Scaly body like a cobra
Ginormous, horrendous wings
Knife-like claws as sharp as daggers
Medusa, Medusa, Medusa.

She is a vile creature
Black protruding tongue
Leathery wings
Snakes dancing like flames
Medusa, Medusa, Medusa.

Porshia Stone (9)
Shakespeare Primary School, Plymouth

Medusa

Hideous, horrible hag
Wings like an eagle
Black protruding tongue
Brown slithery snakes like soap
Medusa, Medusa, Medusa.

Grotesque, gruesome crone
Tusks like a boar
Dagger-like nails
Brown bloodshot eyes
Medusa, Medusa, Medusa.

Sonny Clancy
Shakespeare Primary School, Plymouth

Medusa

Hideous, horrible hag
Sharp knife-like claws just like a grizzly bear
Towering leather wings
Red bloodshot eyes
Medusa, Medusa, Medusa.

The horrendous, slimy crone
Slimy scales that drip with horror
Snakes dancing like flames on top of her head
Tusks that are pointy
Medusa, Medusa, Medusa.

Isabelle Davison (9)
Shakespeare Primary School, Plymouth

Medusa

Hideous, savage Medusa
Hands like knives, blue bloodshot eyes
Snakes dancing like flames
Wings hard like leather
Medusa, Medusa, Medusa.

Medusa, black protruding tongue
Tusks like a boar
Hideous hag, vile creature
Nasty teeth like daggers
Medusa, Medusa, Medusa.

Harvey Lee Sargeant (10)
Shakespeare Primary School, Plymouth

Medusa

Dreadful, beastly, ugly hag
Scaly body like a viper
Knife-like claws as pointy as a shark's tooth
Orange bright eyes
Medusa, Medusa, Medusa.

Terrifying, scary, ugly, old hag
Green scaly body like a dragon
Snakes dancing like flames
Crooked toes
Medusa, Medusa, Medusa.

Angel Tilley (10)
Shakespeare Primary School, Plymouth

Medusa

Hideous, horrible hag
Body covered in bogey-green scales
Big black wings like the Devil's
Bloodshot eyes
Medusa, Medusa, Medusa.

She has a tongue like a viper
Rattlesnake legs with scales
She has serpents for hair
Snakes moving around like fire
Medusa, Medusa, Medusa.

Cameron Godfrey (9)
Shakespeare Primary School, Plymouth

Medusa

Revolting, repulsive, raging hag
Scaly body like a python
Knife-like claws as sharp as a dagger's
Bloodshot eyes as dark as a cave
Medusa, Medusa, Medusa.

Hideous evil creature
Vile old thing
Tusks like a boar
Leathery wings that could make a wind current
Medusa, Medusa, Medusa.

Alfie Dickson (10)
Shakespeare Primary School, Plymouth

Medusa

Ghastly, revolting hag
Green scaly body like a cobra
Knife-like claws as sharp as daggers
Devilish bloodshot eyes
Medusa, Medusa, Medusa.

Horrible, hideous hag
Colossal leathery wings
Sharp knife-like fangs
Medusa, Medusa, Medusa.

Teanna Carey (9)
Shakespeare Primary School, Plymouth

Medusa

Grotesque, horrible, vile, twisted hag
Scaly corpses, savage, merciless, sadistic, callous face
This creature has slinky, sidling, skulking mambas in her hair
Bright blood eyes
Medusa, Medusa, Medusa.

Tangled mambas inserted into her head
Hideous looking face with colossal tusks
Bloody corpses
Medusa, Medusa, Medusa.

Kaiden Michael James Durston (9)
Shakespeare Primary School, Plymouth

Medusa

Horrible, hateful hag
Green scaly skin
Razor-sharp claws like daggers
Red bloodshot eyes with a touch of green
Medusa, Medusa, Medusa.

She has big wings
And very vicious snakes on her head
If you take one step they will bite
Medusa, Medusa, Medusa.

Daisy Sturman (9)
Shakespeare Primary School, Plymouth

Aliens

A ntennae still as sticks
L ots of eyes peeking
I maginary or real? Who knows?
E xperts at flying spaceships
N ever got too close to the sun
S ome don't like being aliens.

Katie Cumberland (8)
Shakespeare Primary School, Plymouth

Medusa

Hideous, horrible hag
Twisted eyes
Scaly body like a shark
Slithery anacondas on her head
Black protruding tongue
Medusa, Medusa, Medusa.

Dawn Kader (10)
Shakespeare Primary School, Plymouth

The Sky At Night

Have you ever looked up at the sky at night
to see the twinkling stars that shine oh so bright.
The moon shimmers bright above them
and shines down upon us all.
It lights up the night sky,
like a large light ball.

Cerys Louise Hanna (8)
Shakespeare Primary School, Plymouth

Medusa

Hideous, repulsive hag,
Claws like daggers,
Wings as black as night,
Tusks like a boar's,
Medusa, Medusa, Medusa.

Tyler Hayman (10)
Shakespeare Primary School, Plymouth

I'm An Alien

A liens
L ive on planets
I s
E veryone an alien?
N ow we are out of this world.

Amy Francis (9)
Shakespeare Primary School, Plymouth

Medusa

Hideous, horrendous hag
Claws like a scalpel
Scales like a monstrous dragon
Red bloodshot eyes
Medusa, Medusa, Medusa.

Josh McCulloch (10)
Shakespeare Primary School, Plymouth

Scamper

Scamper was my cat, she was very fluffy.
She was brown and black and also kind of scruffy.
She loved me and I loved me and I loved her
Especially when she sat on my lap and began to purr.

Hannah Marshall (7)
Shakespeare Primary School, Plymouth

The Space Adventure

Eerie silence cast around my ears,
Only the whoosh of a comet would surprise me,
I held my breath in awe,
The stars shimmered like diamonds,
Wrapping me up – like a blanket,
I risked a glance to my left,
The sun shone deeply into my blue eyes,
Nearly blinding me,
I quickly looked to my right,
Sparkling ants swam in a black hole
Ready to swallow me up,
My memories all flooded back to me
As I took in my surroundings,
I couldn't help my curiosity,
I grew closer and closer until . . .

Maya Bishop (10)
Wylye Valley CEVA Primary School, Warminster

What Am I?

I am bright,
The brightest,
In the night,
I have been visited
Only by a trained few.
They come in odd suits,
They are called humans
As I know them,
They come in a spacecraft,
All white with blue badges,
NASA,
NASA they said,
Their footprints,
Their flags . . .

Hugo Upsall (11)
Wylye Valley CEVA Primary School, Warminster

Space

S hooting stars across the sky
P urple planets as they fly
A nts smaller than the sky
C omets flashing past your eye
E arth spinning around the sun, that's where my adventure began.

Kristian Palmer (11)
Wylye Valley CEVA Primary School, Warminster

Excitement For Everybody

S tars shine so bright tonight,
P assing planets and galaxies,
A rocket flies to a planet,
C atching its eye it sees the moon,
E xcitement for everybody.

The astronauts have finally reached the moon,
Then NASA get involved,
They write letters to the astronauts,
Then the astronauts reply,
Excitement for everybody!

The astronauts have flown back to Earth
And people will cheer and celebrate,
NASA will have to congratulate them
For their amazing experience in space,
Excitement for everybody!

Daisy Dawkins (10)
Wylye Valley CEVA Primary School, Warminster

Out Of This World

O h what sights to see,
U ncountable, there's so many stars,
T he stars are bright like the sun.

O h what a wonderful experience,
F ading into the darkness.

T hat space shuttle passing by,
H ow I'd hate to leave.
I 'm amazed by the sights I can see,
S o many satellites that are not in use.

W ouldn't like to miss a thing,
O pen to everything,
R ound and round there is so much to see,
L ight years away other galaxies await.
D rifting balls of flame shooting across the sky.

Callum Adey (11)
Wylye Valley CEVA Primary School, Warminster

Deep, Dark Space

D eep dark space, what an amazing sight.
E clipse, when the moon covers the sun, in the dead of night.
E ndless journeys, where to go? What will I see?
P erilous trips to see the stars, to take pictures for you and me.

D ancing comets whizzing past me as I'm floating.
A rrow-like stars, shooting past me, as I'm soaring.
R ed, orange, yellow, a huge ball of fire.
K ryptonite, Superman's weakness.

S urprises await me flying through space.
P rizes, glory, being famous everywhere.
A mazing feelings, everyone.
C omets flying, breaking through the atmosphere.
E nd of my journey, what an amazing day!

Elliot Rawlings (10)
Wylye Valley CEVA Primary School, Warminster

The Rocket

Fire-breather,
Planet-orbiter,
Moon-lander,
Space-glider,
High-flyer,
Sky-explorer,
Winged-worker,
Star-observer,
Black hole-avoider,
Galaxy-strutter,
Atmosphere-breaker,
Universe-skimmer,
Ozone-destroyer.

Nathan Rawlings (10)
Wylye Valley CEVA Primary School, Warminster

Space Poem

Twinkling fairy lights covering the sky,
Stars like fairies in space,
Like glitter on a blanket,
Sizzling sun ready to pop,
Like a glitter cannon,
Twinkling stars like silver diamonds,
Bright time portal,
Fairies sparkling their fairy dust,
All I hear is silence,
Blue stars ready to explode,
Colourful stars everywhere you gazed,
Spaceships going around me,
Little aliens everywhere.

Molly Hampson (9)
Wylye Valley CEVA Primary School, Warminster

My Star Life

Stars shine like diamonds in the sky,
Frightens me like a dark shadow in my black tear,
Space is life, day, week, month and year,
And I take a light for my life.
Space is fearless,
Space is worldless,
Space is darkness,
Space is sunless,
When I look up I feel like an ant,
I feel really small in front of a big black hole
And that's how my journey began.

Lee Osment (11)
Wylye Valley CEVA Primary School, Warminster

The World Of Space

If I lived in space I would . . .
Have a barbecue on the sun,
Eat on the Earth,
Swim on Saturn,
Jump on Jupiter,
Fly to the moon,
Sparkle like the stars,
Invent on Venus,
Make a chocolate cake on Mars,
Mop up Mercury,
Play on Pluto.

Toby Oliver Worts
Wylye Valley CEVA Primary School, Warminster

Houston We Have A Problem

There's a fathomless hole in the capsule,
A myriad of vibrant mist in our way,
But before anything else,
We heard the astronaut say,
'Houston, we have a problem . . .'
With abrupt juddering from the back,
With a meteor attack
And a powerful raid of darkness,
We couldn't turn back.
Houston we have a problem
And we're out of this world.

Thomas Benjamin Worts (11)
Wylye Valley CEVA Primary School, Warminster

Deep Into Space

The eerie silence,
Abyss of darkness swallowing me up,
Red and blue stars exploding like bombs being dropped,
The scalding sun casting a shadow across the swirling planets,
Nothing . . .
Fascination burning in my mind,
Flying like a comet around my head,
Stars floating by like a ship in the sea,
Nothing . . .
Just an ocean of death,
Beautiful.

Ava Poolman
Wylye Valley CEVA Primary School, Warminster

Space

Glittery stars above me,
Always twinkle at night,
Sunbathing on Mars,
Like flying as a kite,
Moonwalking on the moon,
Dancing on the sun,
Sliding on Saturn's rings,
While eating a hot cross bun,
Zoom across galaxies,
Eat a star slushie,
Meet an alien that's very pushy.

Poppy Coldwell (8)
Wylye Valley CEVA Primary School, Warminster

Rocket

I'm shiny and bright.
I fly in the sky,
Up in the deep dark space.

I travel fast and silent.
I break the atmosphere,
Up in the deep dark space.

I land on the moon.
People come off me,
Up in the deep dark space.
What am I?

Gieone Bell (11)
Wylye Valley CEVA Primary School, Warminster

Out Of Space

O ur universe is our world
U p in space stars sparkle in the night
T ime passes in the bright sky

O ur life is our time
F ollow the world on a journey of light

S hooting stars light up the night sky
P reparing for the sun to come
A liens dancing around the moon, pushing, shoving over noon
C oldness cramps towards the moon
E mergency landing into space.

Tatum Johnson-Slade (10)
Wylye Valley CEVA Primary School, Warminster

Space Stars

S equins
P lanet
A nother universe dying
C annon
E arth

S izzling sun
T own of aliens
A s shiny as diamonds
R aging diamonds
S hiny silver sequins.

Declan James Michael Carter (10)
Wylye Valley CEVA Primary School, Warminster

Great Space

G lamorous stars
R omantic Mars
E bony never-ending blackness
A quarium for planets
T errible holes

S ucking you up
P hosphorescent lights
A bsorbing you in
C rystal-like stars
E ngaging you forever.

Henning Longlands (10)
Wylye Valley CEVA Primary School, Warminster

Outer Space

O utstanding colours swirling around on a black velvet sheet,
U nbelievable ocean of sparkling stars,
T errible black hole ready to suck me up,
E erie silence cast around my ears,
R olling asteroids tumbling through space.

S tars glittering around me like diamonds on a bracelet,
P eaceful tune dancing round my dizzy head,
A lien world surrounding me,
C rystals in the abyss of space,
E ternal darkness staring me in the face.

Lana Pemberton
Wylye Valley CEVA Primary School, Warminster

Stars

I used to think what stars really are,
Splodges of paint, the light of a car,
What do they actually do?
Make the sky light, instead of dark blue,
Put lots together, they're as big as a planet,
They look like diamonds stuck on a blanket,
My gran told me, a letter was sent,
Out go my ideas, my imagination went,
But I know now, they're part of the sun,
They could be mistaken for seeds on a bun.

Dominic Foote (10)
Wylye Valley CEVA Primary School, Warminster

Consumer

Star stealer
Pitch blacker
Universe vanisher
Earth's doomer
Planet killer
Future's shortener
Silence maker
Astronaut threatener
Light vanisher
A massive black hole!

Alfie (8)
Wylye Valley CEVA Primary School, Warminster

In Space I Saw . . .

In space I saw . . .
A glitter cannon spreading glitter all over the galaxy,
The sun beaming at the Earth,
Diamonds sprinkled all over a black wall.
Spaceships flashing their lights,
Little aliens,
Total silence.
The Earth circles around the sun,
A rocket fired to Mars,
Rings around the planet like an ice ring.

Maddie White (9)
Wylye Valley CEVA Primary School, Warminster

Space

When you first step on the moon it's like a balloon,
The sizzling sun is as hot as an oven,
You can hear twinkling stars,
Black background, dotted colours green, blue and purple,
A dark island with a blue sea of sequins.

Oh look at the sight, it might catch your eye,
Breathtaking abyss hole, ready to swallow you up.
Stars like fresh sparkling snow on a dark height,
It feels like you're rowing in a sea of stars.

Harry Sandy (9)
Wylye Valley CEVA Primary School, Warminster

The Sun

Rocket-melter
Fire-breather
Light-giver
Light-bringer
Planet-grower
Life-bringer
Meteor-burner
Water-evaporator
Eye-blinder.

Leo Moors (10)
Wylye Valley CEVA Primary School, Warminster

Stars

Stars are bright,
Twinkling in the night,
Stars float around the moon,
Whistling a silent tune,
Stars are born,
As sharp as a thorn,
Stars sweep across the skies,
In front of all the children's eyes,
Exploding from time to time.

Rio Oakey (10)
Wylye Valley CEVA Primary School, Warminster

Outer Space

Planets swirled around me in the midnight black,
An eerie silence cupped around my ears,
Comets ruled the skies, zooming from star to star.

Asteroids appeared in the dark abyss of space,
Fizzing like popcorn,
Stars like sparkling ants, filling the sky with light and joy.

Glinting little crystals gazed my way,
As the sun came up and lightened the day.

Izzy Crewe-Read (10)
Wylye Valley CEVA Primary School, Warminster

What Am I?

World-destroyer,
Space-slurper,
Object-stretcher,
Planet-sucker,
Light-consumer,
Human-dissolver,
Comet-crusher.

What am I?

Kai Wilkinson (10)
Wylye Valley CEVA Primary School, Warminster

My Rocket

Up high in the sky
The amazing stars shoot by,
Whistling past me,
Up high in the sky,
My rocket is dazzling,
My eyes closed quickly.

Ellie Nurdin (10)
Wylye Valley CEVA Primary School, Warminster

When I Went To Space

I went to space one day last week and what a sight I saw.
The sparkling stars blinded my eyes,
A sea of planets spun around their leader,
The sun was very close,
It's nearly summer.
I wish everybody down on Earth could come and see.
Maybe we'll send pictures from a satellite.
It's a sight they'll want to see.

Thomas Baker
Wylye Valley CEVA Primary School, Warminster

If I Could Do Anything

If I could do anything I would . . .
Surf in Saturn's rings, watching the sun glow,
Swim in the jewel-like Milky Way,
I'd race on comets, jump from planet to planet,
I'd dance gracefully on the moon,
I'd sing gladly on the sun,
I'd gaze at the world as it slept
And paddle along the ocean of sparkling stars.

Soren Brayne
Wylye Valley CEVA Primary School, Warminster

The Abyss

The endless blanket,
Studded with little glinting diamonds,
Like a guiding light in the foreboding dark.
The amazing nebula,
The super stars,
The gigantic black holes that suck you away into nothingness,
Like a cornerless dimension, full of weird and wonderful things.

Joshua Passmore (10)
Wylye Valley CEVA Primary School, Warminster

Space Poem

Sequins scattered across the sky where aliens live.
Twinkling dragonflies floating in a luminous sea of black.
Stars like gold sparkling diamonds.
The sun like a yellow moon.
The Milky Way is a time portal.
I was amazed when I took my first step on the moon.
It looked like a massive meteor coming towards me!

Zak McLeod-Jones (9)
Wylye Valley CEVA Primary School, Warminster

Out Of This World Poem

A galaxy filled with stars,
Diamonds that shine like a lamp in a pitch-dark haunted house,
Consuming the darkness.
Tons of sparks, too many to count.
A wondrous Milky Way,
That makes you think you need to make endless trips
Before you've absorbed the shimmering, sparkling crystal stars.

Ryan Proud (9)
Wylye Valley CEVA Primary School, Warminster

Space

Space, very empty space,
Stars around me like diamonds in the air,
Silent space, awesome space, black space, silent space,
Odd space, boring space, no air space,
Busy space, alien space and old space!

George Moore (8)
Wylye Valley CEVA Primary School, Warminster

Stars – Haiku

Stars shining bright now,
Like the eyes of a tiger,
I take a deep breath.

Elizabeth Thornton (11)
Wylye Valley CEVA Primary School, Warminster

YOUNG WRITERS INFORMATION

We hope you have enjoyed reading this book –
and that you will continue to in the coming years.

If you're a young writer who enjoys reading and
creative writing, or the parent of an enthusiastic poet or
story writer, do visit our website
www.youngwriters.co.uk. Here you will find free
competitions, workshops and games, as well as
recommended reads, a poetry glossary and our blog.

If you would like to order further copies of
this book, or any of our other titles give us
a call or visit **www.youngwriters.co.uk.**

Young Writers
Remus House
Coltsfoot Drive
Peterborough
PE2 9BF

(01733) 890066 / 898110
info@youngwriters.co.uk